Thierry Arbogast AFC

Cinematographer

The most important task for a cinematographer is to work on the lighting, because it lends ambiance, color and elegance to a movie. You also need to collaborate with the director on the approach to filming, but I think that once you've agreed on the look and how you are going to film, the cinematographer's primary task will be lighting.

This is the reason why I prefer to have a camera operator. I'm always very involved when it comes to framing a shot, or resetting the shot, but afterwards I really devote myself to the lighting.

It is now possible to shoot in the street at night with very little light.

Nikita was a stepping-stone in my career, thanks to Luc Besson. It was the first movie that he entrusted me with and it marks the beginning of my collaboration with him. We quickly reached an understanding when he first expressed his feelings to me about his style of filmmaking. I believe that we have similar tastes when it comes to movies.

Luc appreciates authentic lighting; he likes it when the lighting looks real. But realism is completely relative and we soon moved away from just a realistic approach. We like it when the lighting fits in, when it's clear, but we also want it to bring poetry and magic to the screen.

Shooting in digital makes our work easier, that's for sure. It is now possible to shoot in the street at night with very little light, but from a creative perspective the challenge remains the same. We still need to shape the lighting, because that is what makes cinema look so beautiful and the actors so photogenic.

Sergey Astakhov RGC

Cinematographer

Without a doubt, one of the most amazing cameras developed and produced by ARRI is the ARRIFLEX 35 IIC. The main advantage of this camera is the film gate, which allows the film to move with an extremely high degree of stability. The loop, supported from above and below, partially dampens inertial oscillations; therefore the single claw registration pin can achieve high stability when the film moves, both forwards and in reverse. There was another valuable quality of this camera for the Soviet film industry: we had two perforations—negative and positive. The IIC's pin mechanism would take either, and you could shoot double and triple exposures.

The cinema that's dear to me is the cinema of stories. What I want to see in cinema are intelligible stories that stir the soul and evoke emotion. It's not like entertainment stories haven't interested me; this is my profession, I can do it and it probably needs to be done. But they don't interest me. I am interested in the cinema of sensations, of thought, and then equipment becomes your assistant. Otherwise, it's just toys.

I am interested in the cinema of sensations, of thought.

Volker Bahnemann

Founder of ARRI USA

In the 1970s I was traveling an enormous amount between the East Coast, where our office was located, and the West Coast. Our business in Los Angeles became more and more important because the rental companies started to grow. In that environment I learned an awful lot about the industry and about the application of the equipment. I realized that in the rental houses our equipment was constantly modified; it did not fit the shooting requirements of the motion picture industry. For example, the 35 IIC that we delivered with a handgrip motor was regularly modified into a flat base with an AC motor drive, and the three-lens turret was replaced with what they called a hard front.

It became a very important insight for me that the equipment needs to be built the way it wants to be used, rather than built one way and then sold and used an entirely different way.

When I introduced the need for a new MOS camera in Munich that I wanted to replace the ARRIFLEX 35 IIC, they thought I was absolutely nuts because we were still selling IICs by the truckload, and the question of the salespeople was, "Why would you want to replace such a successful camera?" I made it clear that this camera is never used the way we built it, so let's build a camera that fits the application. And I think we hit a home run, because the ARRI 35 III became instantly the most successful MOS camera in the industry.

The equipment needs to be built the way it wants to be used.

Opening ARRI's first international sales and service subsidiary in this dynamic film market proved to be a historic step, putting us closer to the user and leading to a succession of innovative technologies and new products. A milestone in ARRI's century of remarkable contributions to this industry, which I am fortunate to have been part of.

Bill Bennett ASC

Cinematographer

In the mid-1990s, ARRI offered me a chance to shoot with the first prototype of the ARRIFLEX 435. You don't want to use a prototype as the primary camera of your show, but a buddy of mine was shooting a commercial and they were doing an action sequence downtown at night. When you're doing stunts you want as many angles as possible, so we went down and started shooting on the 435.

Suddenly, a stunt went bad. A car was supposed to come flying over the hill through the air, right towards my camera. But the cannon in the bottom of the car that was supposed to blow and flip it to the side did not blow, and the car was coming straight at me. So we ran and we got out of the way, but the car hit the tripod, which flipped the camera into the air and it smashed onto the ground. You've got to remember that this was ARRI's first hand-built prototype and it probably cost them about a million dollars to build it. So I had to call the management and say, "You know that prototype camera you loaned me? We just hit it with a car." Then there was this long silence on the other end of the phone.

You know that prototype camera you loaned me? We just hit it with a car.

Luckily, I had done a steady test on the camera the day before. I brought it back, they ran another steady test, and it hadn't changed. They just had to replace the magazine

and the matte box because they were destroyed. The engineers, after they'd recovered from the shock of what had happened to their camera, said to me when I met them later, "We would have never dared to throw the camera up in the air and let it land on concrete from ten feet in the air, but we're glad you did it!" Since then, whenever they give me a prototype of something, they always say, "Don't hit it with a car."

Jeremy Benning CSC

Cinematographer

Actually, we wanted to shoot the TV series *The Expanse* with an ALEXA, but we knew we'd be in a lot of cramped spaces and didn't have the luxury of pulling walls out every time we wanted to change angles. Also, our first director, Terry McDonough, was a big proponent of the MōVI, so we needed a camera that could fit in the MōVI.

The ALEXA Mini came out after our first season and now we carry three Minis full-time. You pick it up in your hand

and you realize how tiny it is, and right away you think of all the things you can do with it. We always end up getting stuck in a place where you're up against the wall, in a small space, and what you can do with a smaller camera is usually better than with a bigger camera. The Mini has allowed us to do things that we couldn't do before, because the lens mount is centered in the body, which improves the balance and lets us use heavier lenses.

The Mini has allowed us to do things that we couldn't do before.

The other thing is that we have the full ARRI Lens Data System now. We can drive the focus system internally and strip down the camera even more, and our focus puller can see the readouts on the WCU-4 hand unit. Again, it's another evolution of a better way to work. Our show is VFX-intensive, with two or three hundred visual effects shots per episode, and having that lens data is also a big help for saving time in post. It saves them a couple of hours per shot in the VFX world, so they can do more for less money. I can't imagine not having the LDS now, because it's such a great, simple, streamlined system.

Adam Bentel SASC

Cinematographer

Making films in Africa will always be tricky, due to the modest budgets. This has taught us to embrace a more natural style of filmmaking, which has influenced our approach to how we tell our stories visually. All of our films are ultimately independent films, and the more I work on these intimate, smaller films, the more I discover how important performance is and how important it is to stay out of the space of the actor.

I recently made a film where we were working with non-actors and we had to light a room where our lead, a young girl, is contemplating about being an orphan and moving away from her "grandparents." We're watching this person slowly break down and go through anger, frustration, despair and finally comprehension, and this is all just happening in front of us. It was so raw. We couldn't give her marks, or tell her where to stand; I just had to let her go into darkness. You think to yourself, "I'm lighting with only a Chinese lantern and an M18 bounced through the window outside. But it's Log C on an AMIRA and it's fine, everything is there." Having the scope to do that kind of thing and not impede the performance is just unbelievable.

The more I work on these intimate, smaller films, the more I discover how important performance is.

Steve Beres

VP of Media and Production Operations, HBO

We really strive to get a cinematic experience on television and that comes from the way that we approach content creation. It's much more like developing, creating, shooting and delivering a feature film than it is a traditional television show.

Game of Thrones has this fantasy backdrop that obviously doesn't exist and so needs to be created with a huge amount of visual effects, and to do that on a television schedule is epic. Even 10 years ago we could not have made it. The technology wasn't there yet.

We started *Game of Thrones* with ALEXA before the camera started shipping. We got the first nine bodies off the production line and those all recorded to HDCAM SR tape. Ever since then we have been constantly evolving, along with ARRI, to develop what we think is the very best way to shoot our show. We moved from tape to Codex recorders with JPEG 2000, and from there to recording in-camera ProRes 3.2K, which supports all of the lenses we use and gives us the extra resolution that makes visual effects and compositing much easier.

We have been constantly evolving, along with ARRI.

Game of Thrones basically shoots in up to five countries with up to three units all working simultaneously. Because we are now working with ProRes natively out of the camera, we're able to generate eight hours of dailies a day in just a little more than real time, ready to go to editorial and ready for the crew to review. But also back here in Los Angeles the executives are able to wake up in the morning and review dailies from the previous day, give feedback and have the notes process go back and forth. All of that makes the show so much more efficient and so much more collaborative.

Patrick Blossier AFC

Cinematographer

I don't think of myself as a theorist. I really work on feel, or intuition. For me, the images must be conceived as we create them. That is to say, I come to set being prepared, I know the script by heart and ideally I've had a long period of preparation with the director, even if sometimes we change everything on the first day of shooting. Most importantly, I need to have a good rehearsal with the actors to see how they're going to move and where they're going to go. Then, the framing and lighting are set up simultaneously.

Bizarrely, I don't feel nostalgic about film.

Seeing as I frame and work on the lighting at the same time, the form of the camera is important to me, meaning that I often need to have it on my shoulder, and it must be well positioned. I am still quite traditional in this sense. I haven't taken to these new techniques where you hold the camera at arm's length—these odd systems where you look at a screen. As far as I'm concerned, I look into the viewfinder and the right position for the camera is on my shoulder. The ARRIFLEX 35BL was perfect for this; it was the only one at the time.

When I had to shoot digital, I wasn't familiar with the cameras. I naturally turned to the ALEXA because it actually looks like a camera. My first major experience with it was on the series *The Returned*, for Canal+. Bizarrely,

I don't feel nostalgic about film. I prefer seeing the advantages of digital rather than moaning about the paradise lost of film. Above all, digital cameras allow me to explore the use of very low light, which I wasn't able to do with film. This is an area that really enchants me. With digital, work on set has not really changed, but in postproduction the change is considerable; rediscovering the movie after the edit and then spending three weeks refining your work—that's pretty satisfying.

Matias Boucard

Cinematographer

I enjoy the technical aspect when I master it; I hate not understanding what's going on. It's fascinating that we can be cinematographers and not understand everything, because ultimately there aren't all that many different cameras and lenses, and when you do finally understand something you realize it wasn't so complicated.

But at the same time, I feel like we need to allow ourselves a little bit of the unknown, because it creates an element of doubt. When we have doubt, we take risks, and when we take risks, we create the image. Of course to anticipate problems you need to understand them, you need to master technique. But we learn through experience; we learn on set, so it is always linked to the artistic. You try things, and they work or they don't, but you bounce back and you find a way to get the shot.

When we have doubt, we take risks, and when we take risks, we create the image.

Every year I improve, and the journey is not finished, I hope. I haven't yet fully mastered all of the technique that I should master to be in the position I am in, but it doesn't bother me. I know how to find the information, and I know how to surround myself with people who can manage the technicalities. That's really what the job is about—we work together with other people, solving problems, all in the same direction, creating pictures that tell stories.

Natasha Braier ADF

Cinematographer

The Neon Demon was my first digital film, and I was really scared about shooting on digital. Nicolas Winding Refn is a big digital fan, so there was no way of convincing him to shoot on film. I kind of had to learn throughout the movie how to make the digital as cinematic as possible. In the beginning, I was really trying every possible trick I could think of to make it look more filmic and organic: flaring the lenses and putting Vaseline on them, things like that. By the end of the movie I had my bag of tricks to shoot on digital and I was like, it's fine; I don't have to retire. Thank God they invented the ALEXA—we're going to be okay!

The Neon Demon was a feast of color saturation, and the color was really a big part of the emotional narration. The way that we used it was very different and very new for me. Especially in the second half of the movie, when we go into a crazier world, we separate ourselves from reality and everything is possible, camera-wise and lighting-wise.

I feel like we did poetry, we did music, and that is an amazing experience for me as a cinematographer, to have somebody like Nicolas inviting me to do that without asking for any safety or guarantees—just saying try your craziest idea and if I love it, we go for it. It pushes me to get out of my comfort zone and try going one step further; it takes me to the best work that I can do because I am free to fail and I am free to try, so that's very addictive. It's really great to have the opportunity to team up with someone who is taking you into that territory.

It pushes me to get out
of my comfort zone and try
going one step further.

ALEXA

Garrett Brown

Filmmaker, Inventor

I bought my beloved old ARRIFLEX 35 IIA camera at auction for about $200 and used it on my original prototype to shoot the first Steadicam show reel—the so-called *30 Impossible Shots*. It quickly went as "viral" as a piece of 35 mm film could go in that era. It was seen by Stanley Kubrick, who eventually used it on *The Shining*; by John Avildsen, who was prepping *Rocky*; and by Haskell Wexler, who immediately wanted to try it out on a Keds commercial. It was actually a great running test for the prototype Steadicam, because I had to run flat-out after some girls who were chasing a 14-year-old rock 'n' roller. The results were generally admired and so Haskell booked me for *Bound for Glory*. He devised the first ever Steadicam shot in a film and it was absurdly bold.

Haskell would have me standing on the platform of a Titan crane 30 feet in the air, lowering the crane, stepping off and following David Carradine 300 yards across a field crowded with migrant workers—and back.

I went back and did one more take, with no idea whether it was any good.

I was taught to wait for the tap on my back and, "Okay, you're free," once three big grips had jumped aboard to hold the crane down. We did two takes. One was aborted because a grip—not recognizing my prototype as any sort of camera—began talking to David Carradine. I had little idea whether either take was usable because my early video viewfinder was so

dreadful in full sun, but they gave me a beer at lunch and I went back for one more take. Then I waited around for two days, a stranger among that vast crew, until dailies in a storefront in Stockton.

I showed up to find the whole crew piled in there to see Haskell's amazing stuff. I sat in the very back and finally my shot came up. When it stopped, the crew was silent for a moment and then they all leaped to their feet, clapping, yelling Haskell's name, roaring approval, and with a rush of adrenaline, I realized that something extraordinary had just happened—my existence had just flipped to an entirely different state. You don't get too many of those moments in a lifetime.

Paul Cameron ASC

Cinematographer

My background, like many directors of photography, is 35 mm film. Certainly the transition into digital capture with the ALEXA was kind of an unexpected, very fast transition for feature films, but it's been a good one up to date.

One of the attributes of the TV series *Westworld* is that from the concept phase we treated it like a big movie. There was no discussion about television or the budget or anything. It was about making the right creative choices.

The visual tone of *Westworld* is these two worlds, one is a classic western world and the other is this kind of sci-fi, behind-the-scenes world down below. We wanted the park to feel very authentic; it had to feel like a place that characters would pay a lot of money to visit. And down below we wanted to differentiate it by keeping it a bit darker and dingier, with a corporate and sterile feel.

We decided to shoot film for a more classic cinematic approach. Jumping back into 35 mm film on this project, and specifically using ARRICAM LTs and ARRIFLEX 235s again, was part of what I call a simplification. It took a hundred years to make this medium as perfect and elegant as it is. Shooting on film—the compact nature of it—was great. I like the discipline of metering and taking a film photographically through a lab. It just felt like home again.

I honestly believe that we've got to do our best to keep film as an option, as a creative choice for motion pictures. Film has got its place in history and its place in the future, and I would like to see directors of photography and producers think of it as a viable creative option still, not as a medium that's going out the door.

I honestly believe that we've got to do our best to keep film as an option.

Sudeep Chatterjee ISC

Cinematographer

I am only shooting digital these days and I really enjoy it. I have embraced all the better aspects of shooting digital, and I think my work has improved because of that. But there is one aspect where shooting on film was better: there was a sanctity to the moment when the camera started rolling. You had to be quiet and you had to concentrate. Film material was precious. You only had a certain amount of reels, so everyone took it very seriously. Now you even roll the rehearsals; it has become a little casual. On digital I still shoot the same way that I used to on film. I have an image in my mind and I light accordingly. I try to get the texture I want through lighting and through being involved in the preproduction. You find your look by getting into the art direction and costume, and beyond that there is a lot of control in post.

From a practical point of view I would always choose to shoot digital because I have far more control over the image. I've really learned how to manipulate the image and get exactly what I want.

In 2013 we made a film called *Dhoom 3* and I wanted to shoot it on the ALEXA. At that time you shot digital if you wanted to save money, but this was a big-budget film, the biggest film Bollywood had ever made. My producer and my director were very tentative about it. So I shot a test on 35 mm film, on the ALEXA, and on another digital camera, and I said, "I'll show you all of them and whichever you like, we'll go with that." Interestingly, they picked the ALEXA footage and they said, "Okay, this is film, we like this one."

I would always choose to shoot digital because I have far more control over the image.

James Chressanthis ASC, GSC

Cinematographer, Director

Two film students meet on a street corner in the middle of the Hungarian Revolution. They look at each other and without saying anything, they know what to do: they go up to the film school, they get an ARRIFLEX, and they film the revolution—street battles of young people fighting Soviet tanks. The revolution was lost and they decided to smuggle the footage out to the West. Eventually they came to America, and after 10 years of struggle in Hollywood, they changed American cinema. Those two men were László Kovács and Vilmos Zsigmond.

Once you've risked your life for your art, nothing else compares, and I think that gave both Vilmos and László a bravery and freedom to explore. Nothing would scare them; they could take on any challenge.

> Once you've risked your life for your art, nothing else compares.

They came from a low-budget environment where they had to improvise; they seldom shot on stages or on sets. So they brought that method of shooting to America. The American New Wave hadn't happened yet; they were part of it, bringing stories of real life, shooting on the streets and at real locations. Having small cameras was also part of it, so the ARRIFLEX was the perfect camera for their method of working.

I was very lucky as a student to meet Lázsló Kovács at the American Film Institute, and later I interned with Vilmos

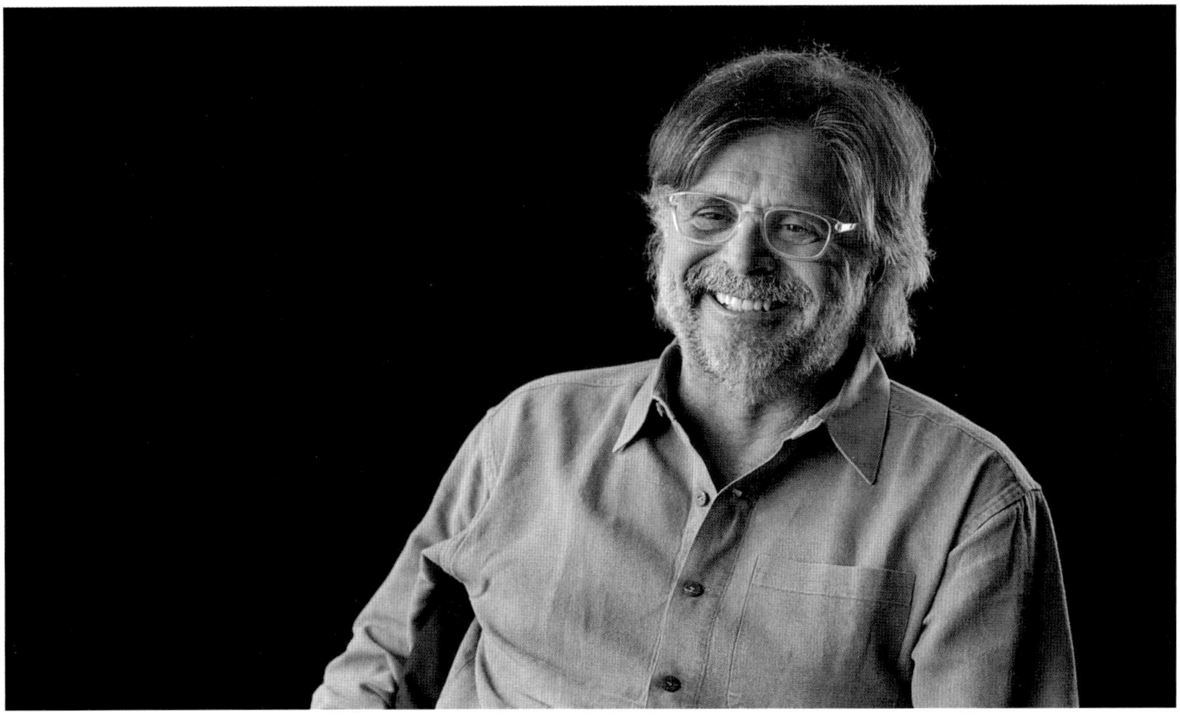

Zsigmond on *The Witches of Eastwick*. I shot second unit for him.

I realized that their friendship and their bond was something very special, and when I saw that Lázsló was becoming ill, I decided to make the double biography *No Subtitles Necessary: Laszlo & Vilmos*, about their lifelong friendship and how it affected cinema.

They were funny. They had a good perspective; they were serious but knew enough not to take themselves too seriously. I miss them both.

Denny Clairmont

President, Clairmont Camera

Haskell Wexler and I were friends. We actually knew each other before I got involved in the feature film business, because my brother and I used to deal in hot rods and sports cars. Haskell sponsored a Can-Am car—very much like an indie-car for road racing—so I knew him from the track when I started to work at Birns & Sawyer Cine Equipment.

Haskell always liked to own his own cameras; he was not a fan of the big rental companies. He had seen or heard about the ARRIFLEX 35BL and he called me to tell me about it, so I got the price sheet and all the information. Haskell came in wearing some old jeans, an old shirt and a funny hat, like how he usually dressed. He asked for me —I was back with the cameras. I came out, we talked and I showed him all the different equipment, and suggested he should buy the camera.

Jack Birns came up, the president of Birns & Sawyer, and said, "You spent 45 minutes with that hippie, isn't that a waste of time?"

So he asked, "Can you please order one for me?" And I said, "Yeah." He wrote a check to Birns & Sawyer for $32,000 and I put it in my shirt pocket. I said goodbye to him and he left. Jack Birns came up, the president of Birns & Sawyer, and said, "You spent 45 minutes with that hippie, isn't that a waste of time?" I replied, "Well, I'm not so sure," and showed him the check. Jack went running up to the glass door and looked out at the parking lot. "Oh my gosh," he said. "That hippie just got into a Rolls Royce."

Richard Crudo ASC

Cinematographer

As a kid I had no idea about being a photographer or a cinematographer, but I do remember being fascinated by light and the different ways it would play out during the day, and through the year. I guess this was a strange obsession, but there's no doubt I understood the emotional impact of what different types of light could deliver, even if I couldn't articulate it at the time. Just imagine when you were off on summer vacation and then August came around. The quality of the daylight started to change; the shadows got a little longer and a little sharper; you could feel the season changing and you knew you were going back to school soon.

The notion of being able to capture that sensation or somehow re-create it—that's exciting. It's the pleasure of preserving a moment, and that's what cinematographers do. Whether it's a dramatic scene with world-class actors or an insert of the magazine on the table, there will never be another instant like that. You've caught it; you've immortalized it. And to then be able to share it with other people, well, that's a tremendously gratifying feeling.

Now, I'm astonished when I light a set and think, "I couldn't read a newspaper here," yet the image is marvelous.

The fabulous thing about today's digital camera is the sensitivity of the sensor. It allows us to use less light than ever before. Just a short time ago we had to carry so many big units—20Ks, 10Ks, all the heavy gear—but we rarely need them anymore. Now, I'm astonished when I light a set and think, "I couldn't read a newspaper here," yet the image is marvelous. It's pretty amazing stuff, really. And as it allows us to do our jobs more creatively and efficiently, it bodes tremendously well for the future.

Roger Deakins CBE, ASC, BSC

Cinematographer

A number of cinematographers criticize the process of digital and having monitors on sets; they say it has taken away the mystery of the black box, whatever that is. I welcome the lack of mystery. It has made it so much easier to talk with the director about a scene and say, "If we stage it like this, I can put them against this window. We could silhouette them in this wide shot, and then we have a cross light for the close shots." I can actually explain it and they see it on the monitor, so they're not going to sit in dailies and go, "I know you said silhouette, but I thought I might be able to see their faces."

Don't get me wrong—I absolutely love film! I have shot film for 40 years without regret, but there are so many advantages to digital. There are things that I can do photographically that would have been very difficult, if not totally impossible, on film. For instance, there is a scene in *Prisoners* where Hugh Jackman's character is stuck in a hole that is blocked off with a plank of wood, and it is night. How do you light that? How do you shoot a sequence like that? Denis Villeneuve and I were talking about it and he said, "What if he's got a cigarette lighter?" If that had been film, I wouldn't have even gone there, but we basically shot this scene with a cigarette lighter, and it was great. You've got so much more in your negative before the image falls apart. That's a simple example, but it's about taking those kinds of risks. Even if you had got some sort of an

I can actually explain it and they see it on the monitor.

image with film, it would have been a compromise in image quality and you'd probably have had a sleepless night or two.

It's a bit of a flippant comment, but it's nonetheless true: when you shoot on film—I don't care how experienced you are—there is always that nagging doubt that you went too far with something, or maybe you didn't go far enough.

Benoît Debie SBC

Cinematographer

The Wim Wenders movie *Every Thing Will Be Fine* was my first 3D film. I really liked doing 3D. At the time, we were using ALEXA M cameras, because the Mini didn't exist yet. Wim wanted a relatively subtle 3D movie; he didn't want to disturb viewers with the 3D. As for me, I also learned a lot; it was a different approach to framing and lighting.

We have just finished shooting *Submergence*, the most recent 2D film by Wim Wenders. Wim decided to shoot the whole movie with handheld cameras, which was fairly new to him. Usually he likes long takes, but in this instance he really wanted to change his style in a radical way. So we shot the entire film with two cameras, which was quite complicated, even for me, because there were a lot of relatively difficult scenes when it came to the actors. We used two ALEXA Minis with small and lightweight Cooke lenses; this enabled us to be flexible in our filming style, which was quite enjoyable. It was my first experience with the ALEXA Mini and I was very impressed with the degree of comfort when working with these handheld cameras.

Wim decided to shoot the whole movie with handheld cameras, which was fairly new to him.

I was proud to be the colorist on *Carol*.

John Dowdell

Colorist

Digital intermediate (DI) is a fairly recent phenomenon; it started when we could scan movie film into a digital file and do all the color corrections digitally, generally in a theater environment, and then shoot with the ARRILASER back to film.

I was proud to be the colorist on *Carol*, working with the beautiful Super 16 cinematography of Ed Lachman. Each day, the exposed film would be shipped from Cincinnati, where they were shooting, and we would scan the dailies. The ARRISCAN has a dailies-type setup where it runs the film a little faster, so everything would be scanned and color graded overnight, then sent back to Ed in Cincinnati. We also made files for the editor, and when editing was finished, we went back to the ARRISCAN and this time rescanned everything at 3K resolution.

At this point, Ed and Todd Haynes, the director, came in. We all worked on the color together. Todd had what's called the look book, and this was just tear sheets and photos of the 1950s that created the patina and the look. So we would actually look at the book and then look up at the screen as the image was being projected, looking back and forth and tweaking things: we'd make it a bit more muted, or emphasize this or that color a little bit, until we were all happy with the result.

Christopher Doyle HKSC

Cinematographer, Director

The difference between filmmaking in Asia and the West is cultural. In the East we have Buddhism; we have mandala. You look at something and then you focus on it, you meditate on it and you go towards the center of the idea. I like this Asian process a lot, which is about finding the film rather than creating the film.

Up until recently in Chinese filmmaking, you didn't have the budget to do much. You couldn't change the color of a wall. You certainly couldn't take away a wall, so you took what you had and tried to make it into something valid for you. I might walk into a room and say, "Oh, that wall is blue, so maybe blue is one of our themes." It is your attention to those possibilities that forms your own style.

In Asia we move fast, we are in very tight spaces; we do not have a big crew. So the organic nature of the camera is very important to me, the balance and how it feels. I have done so many films handheld, and it's only because of the cameras. In general, you have much more flexibility because the cameras now respond so well and you can tweak things in postproduction. It liberates us to do things that we could not have done otherwise. The danger is that you get obsessed with this technology and what it can do, as opposed to what it means. If technology can help us to expand the language, that's its greatest use, but if all it does is suggest everything is possible then you get lost, and then your filmmaking and your voice will just be blurred.

If technology can help us to expand the language, that's its greatest use.

Whether it's a light, or an angle, or the way in which the camera moves, or a technical innovation, if it gives us an experience that is valid and exciting, and pushes us to respond, then of course we should embrace it. This is the whole function of what we do. It is only through that moment where the camera engages you and shows you something you have not seen before—that is cinema to me.

Tom Fährmann BVK

Cinematographer

For me, the DP role is tremendously satisfying. Working behind the camera just brings me to life. I feel totally different from the way I feel in normal life, it's like this kind of energy explodes inside of me that I never have otherwise.

I really focus on the content because I know that once I've understood the film, when I'm feeling it, then the shots just take care of themselves. When someone offers me material, the first thing I do is take myself away and read the whole script in one sitting. I don't think about how it should be shot, I just want to hear the story first of all. Do

I find it interesting? Is it exciting? Do I believe the dialogue? Do I believe the characters?

These days I work in digital. My last analog film was *Pope Joan*; it had a really clear visual concept. The film takes place in the 9th century and tells the story of Johanna, a simple girl with no access to education who rises to become pope. We wanted to use the visual language to represent the development of the character, of her intellect and abilities. We shot the start—which takes place in a bleak village environment where the houses don't even have proper windows—with a moderately framed handheld camera. This contrasts with the images of the huge, cathedral-like rooms of medieval Rome, full of gold and light and sun.

The relationship between a cameraman and his camera is something very special.

Every film has its own visual world that the director and cameraman work on together. Ideally, the director and cameraman are like two knights in a battle, fighting back-to-back together. I know the other guy's behind me and I can focus totally on the images, and because I've got his back, he can give all his attention to the actors. If everything works out okay, the partnership is brilliant. Then I can go pedal to the metal. That's when I can get on, and everything just works.

Pedro Farkas ABC

Cinematographer

Many times I have asked myself why it was I became a cinematographer, and I do not know. I could have been an architect, or other things, but photography was always in my life. My grandfather and my father were photographers, and they had a photographic store in Brazil. Even if I don't know exactly when or why I decided to do it, I love light, I love stories and I love films, so I am very happy. Cinematography is the best work in the world and they pay you for this. It is a pleasure.

The Brazilian film industry is very weak. We do not have a domestic market so we need money from the government to stay alive. Now it is becoming more realistic because all the TV stations have to buy Brazilian productions. So it is beginning to walk on its own two feet.

I think in the future people will see films on the computer and television at home. My daughters, they see a film and they talk on the phone—they do everything together. This is different from me. When you go to the cinema and the curtain opens, it's so magical. You need time to see a film. You need silence. Even in my house, when I want to see a film, I put the lights off and close the door. It is like a dream.

I love light,
I love stories and
I love films, so
I am very happy.

Jon Fauer ASC

Cinematographer, Publisher

In the mid-1970s, I was working at Vision Associates in New York and one of my jobs as staff cameraman was taking care of their ARRI cameras. After every shoot I would make a trip from Manhattan to Woodside, where ARRI was located, to have the cameras maintained. That's where I met a young gentleman with a moustache and bell-bottoms named Volker Bahnemann. I would sit down in Volker's office, where he would grill me on the business and also give me advice. One of his great pieces of advice was, "Jon, you should buy equipment." So in a single week in 1978 I got married, bought an apartment, went freelance, and bought my first ARRIFLEX 16SR camera. Over the rest of my career I bought pretty much every camera that ARRI came out with.

I was always a geek about technique and technology. I had a degree in art history, but always wanted to learn how things worked. At that time the cameras came with basically no instruction manuals, unless you spoke really good German, so I wrote notes to myself and to my crew as to how we should use them. Those notes eventually led to the first book that I did, the *16SR Book*, and I went on to write a book for every camera that I owned.

Over the years, Volker and I were a good team, working on some film projects together. The most fun was a massive two-year project called *Cinematographer Style* in the mid-1990s, where we interviewed 110 cinematographers around the world. The film was about this emerging new method

We would dream up these incredible shots and it got to the point where if you could imagine something you could *almost* shoot it, and some years later you *could* shoot it.

of shooting on film, scanning it with an ARRISCAN, and then going back out to film with an ARRILASER. It was an early stage in the digital age of film. It was also about the craft and the art of why films look the way they do.

Throughout my career, and I mostly did commercials, the style I adopted was heavily influenced by the equipment. We would dream up these incredible shots and it got to the point where if you could imagine something you could *almost* shoot it, and some years later you *could* shoot it. And that was made possible by the equipment.

Bill Feightner

CTO, Colorfront

Before ARRI got into the game, we had developed our own laser film recorder. Then ARRI came up with some really good, state-of-the-art new way of harnessing lasers to make a practical film recorder. The approach that ARRI was taking was much simpler and a lot of it was automatic, so we jumped on that and abandoned our efforts. And it was really the same story with the scanner—we had gone through a number of different scanners, but the ARRISCAN was much higher quality and let us grab all the information on a 35 mm film frame.

We Were Soldiers, with Dean Semler as the cinematographer and Mel Gibson as the director, was—to my knowledge—the first film that was 100 percent digital intermediate, without any laboratory touch-up or laboratory timing. We were really under the gun and everybody was looking at us. We had to chase the mainstream photochemical process to prove ourselves, and I think we were very successful. I remember sitting in the digital intermediate room with Dean and saying, "We've been adjusting timing lights, which is what you do photochemically, but look what else we can do." And once we showed him, I think that was the beginning of the end; we had opened up the Pandora's box of all these additional tools.

Film has a nice look but there are many, many possible looks in the world.

Film has a nice look but there are many, many possible looks in the world. We reached a point where we inversed the process, where we developed completely new and unique digital looks, and we made the film process chase the digital look. Then as we moved ahead, the film—in terms of the screening or in the cinema—fell away to the more efficient digital process, and there we are.

Gavin Finney BSC

Cinematographer

I was asked to shoot *Terry Pratchett's Hogfather* for Sky Television. It was going to be a very big shoot with a lot of stage work and a lot of visual effects; we wanted the best camera, but we also wanted to shoot digitally. We had heard about a new ARRI digital camera called the D-20. It had not actually been released at this point, but what we saw made us think it could be perfect for our show. The images just looked beautiful; they looked similar to 35 mm film. We also did tests on blue screen and green screen, and the visual effects supervisors pulled brilliant keys. They thought this would work very well for us and in fact *Hogfather* went on to win the BAFTA for visual effects.

It was a big jump, as we were amongst the first to be using the D-20. Our decision was driven in large part by our trust in Bill Lovell of ARRI Rental and his extraordinary knowledge of digital systems in general, and the D-20 in particular. He was an infectiously enthusiastic man and a great teacher. Bill was completely straight and honest about the capability of whatever he was talking about. Without that kind of trust and belief in Bill, we would not have gone ahead.

When we were using that camera, we built a set that was meant to be an ice castle but in fact was made out of polystyrene blocks coated in wax, and to make it glow I had to use a huge amount of light. It was a very hot summer and the set itself had started to melt; the wax covering the polystyrene blocks was starting to drip off. We could not physically touch the camera—it was too hot. Still it just kept on happily turning over, with no problems at all. We did not tell Bill that we had roasted one of the only D-20s in the world, but it was fine, it just carried on going.

Our decision was driven in large part by our trust in Bill Lovell of ARRI Rental.

For me good lighting is lighting that you don't see, that tells a story really well.

Mo Flam

Gaffer

I don't come from the Hollywood thing; my first experiences with filmmakers and lighting were on a small scale on location in New York. One of them was on a very low-budget TV movie for German television called *Dear Mr. Wonderful*, shot by Michael Ballhaus. I had watched all the Fassbinder movies at film school and suddenly there I was, working with a cinematographer who had done films I admired, so I was very happy.

Michael had a very simple approach: he was just trying to get good images, telling the story without being elaborate. On location he wouldn't light every centimeter of the image, it was more expressionistic or stylized, and the stylization made it more real because it wasn't overly lit; it didn't look like a studio, it looked like a location. It wasn't as flat as Hollywood lighting, and that's why the European cinematographers did very well in America—because they weren't making it all bright and perfect and glossy. Even today that style is respected and now everybody is doing it.

For me good lighting is lighting that you don't see, that tells a story really well. Maybe we'll enhance the story, add a mood, but we don't want to draw attention to the lighting. We want to make it kind of hyper-real—taking the reality and enhancing it a little bit, increasing the contrast. Michael Ballhaus just had that approach and I was lucky to work with him.

Takehiko Fukae

Cinematographer

Choosing the right light and the right lens has the biggest impact on the image. Anamorphic is interesting because it is not an everyday experience. When I was going to try the Master Anamorphic lenses and their flare sets, my first thoughts were of the paintings of Cézanne. He used multiple perspectives in his paintings, and he made the third dimension two-dimensional. He also put a lot of information in one single picture. Shooting anamorphic without the flare sets is like painting in the style of Cézanne.

When I tried the flare sets, it was like suddenly being set free.

When I tried the flare sets, it was like suddenly being set free. It felt similar to American pop art, such as Jackson Pollock's action paintings; there is the same mixture of controllable and uncontrollable factors. When you use a lens that flares like that, you can express an emotional atmosphere and a rich halation. It's so interesting and I found it very exciting. You couldn't create the same effect in postproduction.

James Gardner CSC, SASC

Cinematographer

One of my favorite films was *The Adventures of Yellow Dog*, which I did with Phillip Borsos in the mid-1990s. We spent seven months out in the islands around Vancouver doing that. It was all outside, going up rivers, down rivers, in helicopters, on boats. We had ARRIFLEX cameras and you couldn't really look after them or put them in their boxes. They were up in slings and on lifts—it was tough for them, but I can't remember anything going wrong.

The look of the film was just a naturalistic one, making the countryside look as good as we could and showing this young boy out in the wild. We didn't have any of today's fancy DIT guys or color grading. What you ended up getting is what you got. You had to do it all on set, outside.

The transition to digital was not just a transition away from film cameras, but also away from different types of film stock to help you create different images and looks. In the beginning, everybody was trying to make the ALEXA look like film, which it doesn't exactly, and never will do. But you can shoot in such low light it's unbelievable, so you have to adapt your lighting. It's similar to that stage in

We had ARRIFLEX cameras and you couldn't really look after them or put them in their boxes.

the film days when it moved away from Hollywood lighting into big, softer washes of light, like David Watkin and the Wendylight he created, which we all started carrying around.

Birgit Guðjónsdóttir BVK, IKS

Cinematographer

ARRI's digital cameras are simple. I can operate them intuitively and I don't need to be a computer expert. On set, I don't have time to worry about the technology; I want to be able to use it like a pencil, so that I can concentrate completely on making pictures and telling stories.

I need to get close to what's happening with the camera, close to the story; I need to catch the spark. And it isn't necessarily just about getting glossy pictures. On the contrary, sometimes the best pictures are dirty and blurry. It's their inner power that counts. The ideal for me is pictures that inspire viewers and make them think.

A few years ago I shot a TV film in Munich called *Zappelphilipp*, where a nine-year-old boy played the leading role. I thought it was important to get the camera down to a height of 1.3 meters, and I was determined to shoot handheld. So I needed a small camera and I chose the ALEXA M. It was ideal in terms of size; the only small issue was that the cable on the back kept poking me in the stomach. I took the problem to ARRI, and the way they responded was brilliant. Someone from the technical department came to visit me on set immediately, watched for a bit, and asked what we needed the camera to do. Then they made it happen. Today, we have the ALEXA Mini, and I maintain that I was partially responsible for its development. I'm very happy about that.

I took the problem to ARRI, and the way they responded was brilliant.

Anette Haellmigk

Cinematographer

I first came to the United States with Jost Vacano to work on *Robocop* as the 1st AC. By *Total Recall* I had become the camera operator, and then on *Starship Troopers* I was the second unit DP. I shot second unit on more Paul Verhoeven films after that, which was fantastic, but I think the world was not ready for female DPs yet, especially the feature film world.

When I saw the first trailers for *Game of Thrones* I immediately thought, "I want to work on that show." Maybe it has to do with growing up in Germany, where tales of knights and princesses were very much part of my childhood. I was asked to join them on season three and when I got there, I was like, "Oh, now we're in the big

league, am I going to be able to do this?" So I had the shivers at first, but I've now shot four seasons—more episodes than anyone.

In terms of image quality, I'm looking for the most latitude you can get. *Game of Thrones* lives in the shadows, so you need a lot of information there, without having to over-expose and lose detail in the highlights. Our production travels to many countries; the landscapes and climates vary widely. We take the cameras to 100 °F in the sun and then we take them to big snow in Iceland, and the ALEXAs have never failed. They are workhorses that you can just completely rely on.

When I saw the first trailers for *Game of Thrones* I immediately thought, "I want to work on that show."

Jan Harlan

Director, Producer

I started working with Stanley Kubrick in 1969, on *Napoleon*. This film never happened and instead we did *A Clockwork Orange.* In those days we filmed with an ARRIFLEX 35 IIC in a blimp; after that it was the ARRIFLEX 35BL. The technicians at Arnold and Richter were always incredibly helpful and Stanley stayed with ARRI all the time until his last film, *Eyes Wide Shut.* For Stanley, Munich was the center of the technical aspect of filmmaking.

He loved the equipment and he liked to be mobile. He did a lot of filming handheld and he was very good at it. The small and light IIC was perfect for this.

Stanley liked to buy his own cameras and lenses, but he wouldn't just order a lens. We would get five lenses, all the same—let us say a 50 mm f/2—and test them on a grid. While theoretically you could say they are all the same, they are not, there are slight differences. We spent a lot of time on this, it was typical for his style of meticulous filmmaking—all aspects mattered.

Stanley would have adored the way modern digital cameras work.

The understanding with his crew was clearly that he was in charge, whether it was the editor, or the DP, or the focus puller. And they respected him because he was competent, so there was never a conflict.

Since he was always at the cutting edge of technology with everything, even in the office with his computers, Stanley would have adored the way modern digital cameras work. Not only because he could instantly see what he has shot, but to be freed of laboratories would also have been a great blessing. Another development he would have applauded is the long and excellent television series. To condense a big novel into two and a half hours of screen time often forces too many compromises. So, now would be the time to do *Napoleon* properly. I am very sad that he is no longer with us.

Agnieszka Holland

Director

I remember that in communist Poland, after I finished film school, the only sound cameras available were these huge and very noisy cameras made just after the war. Then there came the ARRIFLEX 35BL, which was small enough to use handheld. Everybody wanted this camera and I dreamed of using it handheld while still recording direct sound, but I wasn't important enough to get it. So I bought a bottle of vodka, went to the guy who was responsible for taking care of the camera, and drank with him. Eventually, he gave it to me for a couple of days. Ever since then, ARRI cameras have been my dream cameras.

I bought a bottle of vodka, went to the guy who was responsible for taking care of the camera, and drank with him.

Kyung-Pyo Hong

Cinematographer

My first film was a low-budget movie called *Fly Low*. I filmed it with an ARRIFLEX 16BL that I had bought in Los Angeles: a used one, with a zoom lens. In the very first scene of the movie, the character rides in a taxi on the way to school. We had to shoot it at a certain time of day, since I needed to capture the reflected image of the actor in the window. That scene was the start of my career as a cinematographer and a prelude to my lighting style in the coming years.

I had to sell the 16BL right after finishing *Fly Low*, as I didn't have enough money. How poor was I at that time, to sell off that camera! I'd love to get it back, but I can't find where it went. It's the most memorable camera of my life.

When a project is finished I always take a break, doing nothing for a week, and the best way I can relax is by watching lots of movies. I try to utilize the time to learn new techniques and keep myself motivated. I always hope to work on a new style of movie and come up with a fresh look for my next job. There were times I failed to achieve that. There were times I did not like the outcome. But at least, during the productions, I always try my best to achieve it.

How poor was I at that time, to sell off that camera!

Mai Iskander

Cinematographer, Director

My dad's side of the family is Egyptian, and my aunt had been involved in a garbage village community on the outskirts of Cairo for over a quarter of a century. I was volunteering there and in 2005 I started working on a documentary called *Garbage Dreams*, which follows three teenage boys growing up in the village. The garbage village is home to 60,000 Zabbaleen, known as garbage people, who collect Cairo's garbage and recycle 80 percent of

everything they collect. When their community is suddenly faced with the globalization of its trade, each of the teenage boys is forced to make choices that will impact his future and the survival of his community.

I shot the film over the course of four years on my PD150, but right before the last shoot, which was going to be the last scene in the film, the camera went down. I called the only person I knew in Cairo and he said he had one camera, but he hadn't used it in a while; it was an old ARRIFLEX 16SR. So we went all the way to his studio near the pyramids to get the camera. The driver I was with was very eager to get going and I knew that once we got back into the garbage village the electricity wasn't always reliable, so I locked myself in the bathroom to charge the batteries. I stayed in there for like an hour and a half, so he couldn't rush me; I don't know what he thought I was doing. I shot the last scene—which was a wedding in the middle of the garbage village—with the 16SR and it looked really nice to have that contrast with the video world.

I locked myself in the bathroom to charge the batteries.

When I made *Garbage Dreams*, I realized that being both the director and the director of photography really allows you to be compact and to create an intimate relationship with the people you are filming. It lets you be very mobile, very in the moment. I just got really used to that way of working.

Peter James ASC, ACS

Cinematographer

I was hopeless at school. I'm dyslexic and so I didn't go anywhere. When I was 15 I left school and a cousin, who was an author, recommended that I get into photography, because I was really interested in doing that. He had contacts with a studio, so I got a summer job there. I loved it from the very first day and I thought, "This is it, this is what I want to do." Mum was tucking me into bed and said, "How was it at work today?" And this little 15-year-old kid said, "Well, I want to win the Oscar for cinematography." I still haven't won the Oscar for cinematography, but I had a focus in my life and that was to be a good cinematographer.

In 1970 I won the top Australian prize for cinematography, called the Milli, for the first time. I was only 25 and that was a huge boost for me because the prize that year was a Lufthansa flight to Munich and a week at ARRI. For somebody who had basically never been out of the country, getting a trip like that was fantastic.

I timed it for Oktoberfest, which was–I thought–very smart. Going into the German factory in Munich was a bit of an eye-opener: very precise, very old school. Everybody had dustcoats on and it was very formal. People were extremely friendly and accommodating; we had lots of celebrations and went off to the beer tents every night. After about three days of this I couldn't work out why my cheeks were hurting; it was because I was smiling so much, drinking copious amounts of beer and having a great time.

The prize that year was a Lufthansa flight to Munich and a week at ARRI.

Geng Ji

Director of Technology, August First Film Studio

August First Film Studio was founded by the Chinese state in 1952. Today, it produces feature films, military education films and television series. Since the founding of the studio we have had over 100 different cameras. From the early ARRIFLEX models to the modern ALEXA, ARRI cameras have been the main workhorses and have contributed a lot to our productions.

One legendary film produced by August First Film Studio was the trilogy *Decisive Engagement*, in the early 1990s. The sheer scale of the movie was unprecedented in the history of Chinese war films. It took three years to make and involved around five million people, with the most epic scene requiring more than ten thousand cast and crew. We set up an aerial shot on a jet and flew over the crowd; other scenes involved extensive pyrotechnics, sometimes taking a week to set up. Nowadays this kind of scene can be done with CGI and we would never see productions using practical effects on that scale anymore.

We were taught that these cameras were our weapons; we should protect them with our lives.

At that time cameras were very expensive and precious items of equipment. We were taught that these cameras were our weapons; we should protect them with our lives. Near the end of the production of *Decisive Engagement*, a colleague of mine insisted on carrying the ARRI camera himself while descending from a mountain. It was monsoon season, so the mountain road was wet and slippery. He suddenly fell and rolled downhill; he managed to hold the camera tightly in his arms, but both he and the camera got knocked about on the rocks. The fall looked quite serious and we were all very concerned. It turned out that the camera only suffered a few minor dents; we tested it and everything worked fine.

Zeng Jian

Cinematographer, Editor

I always keep an eye on the latest developments and camera system upgrades, researching how I can take advantage of new products and features.

For *Blind Message* I wanted to use a highly compact camera because the locations were very confined spaces, so we had the very first ALEXA M shipment in Asia. It was very handy and easy to use, and felt like a 16 mm camera on my shoulder.

There was a scene in a barbershop with a lot of pink light, where one actor charges in and a fight breaks out. The fight moved from inside to the street outside and it was all shot in one long take. We went through many lighting situations and I remember we even changed the ASA rating in the middle of the take. We were always pushing the limits.

When shooting interiors I prefer to use practical lights that can be included in the shot, such as sodium lamps and tungsten lamps. When it comes to high-power lights I recently started using ARRI SkyPanels. I can add different gel effects simply by entering a number on these digital lights.

In the barbershop I kept the original interior lighting, which was a mix of different-colored fluorescents. We only enhanced the existing lighting in selected areas. It was wintertime, so the owners were using an oscillating electric heater and we incorporated this as well, which added some

When shooting interiors I prefer to use practical lights that can be included in the shot.

red color. There was an intimate scene between a couple that was lit entirely with this heater. Sometimes the heater turned to the actors at just the right moment and then faded away gently, which was an interesting effect.

Hardwrick Johnson

Senior VP, ARRI Rental New York

In 1962 I moved from Florida and was employed at Camera Service Center as a porter messenger. I had to travel by subway to make small deliveries of things like lenses or wedge plates. Never having been in a big city like New York, I didn't have a clue about the subway system, so I was constantly getting lost. After three months, my boss put me in the camera room.

Downstairs there was a lighting and grip company called Charlie Ross. Every day on my lunch hour I would check out their lighting and grip equipment; it took me about three years to learn it all. After that I decided to speak to my boss about starting our own lighting and grip department. He said, "Let me think about it." Three weeks later, he gave me the okay and signed the requisition for me to order all the equipment that I needed, which turned out to be $33,000.

To get business, I frequented a lot of bars where I knew film crews were hanging out in the evenings.

To get business, I frequented a lot of bars where I knew film crews were hanging out in the evenings. Eventually, I made good contacts with them and we began to get commercials business. We became the biggest lighting house in New York City. In around 1968 we got the ARRIFLEX 35 IIC cameras and they became a big part of our rental. The next camera that really put us on the map was the ARRIFLEX 35BL—everybody loved that camera.

I became friends with Spike Lee and we were able to do *Malcolm X,* which was our biggest feature film back in the early 1990s. From then on, I did all of Spike Lee's films until *Inside Man*.

We had some tremendous personalities and that makes a big difference. They knew the clients and the clients knew them, so it was very easy to do business. We need to keep that—to build up personalities.

Mahmoud Kalari

Cinematographer

In 1999 I shot *The Wind Will Carry Us* and it was a very special experience. Abbas Kiarostami was completely different from other directors—his style of directing and storytelling, where he never wrote the story completely. Sometimes he knew exactly what it was he wanted, and sometimes he tried to find it. He did not talk about the camera or the lenses; he just said, "All of your equipment must fit in my car." So we got one camera, an ARRIFLEX 35BL 2, with a set of five lenses, one tripod, two or three magazines and our film stock.

For about 70 days we went on that journey with him and had no idea what would happen. We were shooting in the Kurdistan region of Iran; sometimes we drove 10 kilometers and sometimes almost 100 kilometers to get a single shot. One of my assistants, Behzad Dourani, was the main actor in the movie. He would load the magazine, put up the tripod, and then go and act in front of the camera. It was like a documentary, but it was not a documentary.

Sometimes we drove 10 kilometers and sometimes almost 100 kilometers to get a single shot.

We would drive around in Kiarostami's car, with the camera ready. He was driving himself, looking at the people on the side of the road, and suddenly he would stop and say, "Okay, ready." I would put the camera on my shoulder and the sound man would get his microphone out. In one location Kiarostami was asking people, "This village is not on the map and there is no sign on the road, so how can you find this place?" They replied, "I live here," or "What do you mean?" Kiarostami was not satisfied with these answers, and I asked him, "What is the answer you want?" "I do not know." "So how do you know that this is not the right answer?" He continued asking people until one guy answered, "We never leave this village and so we are never obliged to find the way back." "This is the answer," said Kiarostami. It was a very different style of filmmaking.

Fariborz Kamrani

Managing Director, Iran Telekala

It was my late dad, Seyfedin Kamrani, who started our collaboration with ARRI in 1948. He was quite a pioneer, in terms of looking for new technologies, and he had vivid memories of his first meeting with Mr. Arnold and Mr. Richter. He imported the full range of ARRI products into Iran, from lights and cameras to laboratory equipment like developing machines and printing machines. Throughout his career, ARRI was one of the main companies that my dad cooperated with, so I have known those four letters all my life.

ARRI was one of the main companies that my dad cooperated with, so I have known those four letters all my life.

Our digital restoration work was initiated about seven years ago. There was talk about whether Iranian archival work should be sent for restoration outside the country. In the end we decided to purchase an ARRISCAN, and the first job that we did was the black-and-white film *The Night It Rained*, from 1967. It is one of the most famous Iranian documentaries. The damage was extensive and we only had two people to work on it, so it took us a year and three months to restore this 45-minute film. The result was astonishing and the director, Kamran Shirdel, was invited to take a look. His first impression was that it looked too good! He said, "Please introduce some slight jitters or other effects, little things that would still give a vintage feeling." But he was quite amazed at what had been done.

I'm proud to have created the capability to restore films in my home country. The ARRISCAN gives us the possibility to get the maximum out of our old material, reviving these old films and getting back our heritage.

Judith Kaufmann BVK

Cinematographer

Of course digital filming has indisputable advantages: the light sensitivity, the possibility to view and edit material immediately—all of that creates flexibility, but a lot has also been lost along the way. I miss the actual film, the grain, the structure, the depth, the overexposure, and the sound during filming. I miss the care that was needed, because you knew there was only a certain amount of material available and it was very expensive, so you had to make decisions in advance. This perceived limitation is not necessarily a bad thing.

For me, film was always ARRI. It began when I was a 19-year-old assistant. There was the loading of the magazine—I always timed myself with a stopwatch, to see how quick I could be with the various magazines. You really developed a relationship with the devices; those cameras were my heroes. To me, they were what pop stars are to others. All those beautiful surfaces, the shutters, the reflectors—all the individual parts of the camera, which you knew inside out; you experienced it as a sensual relationship. And then later, as a camerawoman, it always filled me with a mixture of magic and respect.

Those cameras were my heroes. To me, they were what pop stars are to others.

It takes a long time simply to be able to work intuitively, instead of reverting to the tried and true methods. Once you've spent years solving all kinds of problems, you lose the fear of failing and gain the freedom to try new things. I'm still curious and interested in new ways of working, because that for me is the core of our work: the perpetual search for the right expression.

Darius Khondji ASC, AFC

Cinematographer

I like cameras that register in a sharp way, sensors that give a lot of presence to the characters in the foreground or to far-off landscapes, and I like the scan of a negative to be done in the most perfectly sharp way. But then the image itself—I like to give it a specific look that is not necessarily sharp, but more about atmosphere. That is why I love softer glass for lenses. I am always looking for old lenses, and even when I shoot digital, I prefer shooting with older lenses.

I like fog, a misty atmosphere at night, and winter light during the day. I love William Turner, the painter, for his atmosphere and his daylight. I like the sun behind the clouds. When I was with Bong Joon-ho in Korea preparing his film *Okja*, we were talking about the clouds, the Korean landscape and cityscape, and how in wintertime the sun is always very nebulous behind the clouds.

I like confusion and dreamy states. But I say that, and then I shoot a movie where everything needs to be surgically sharp, and that is beautiful too. There are different sorts of cinema. The moment you say this is how you do things, you then realize you have to do the opposite on your next film and it becomes your passion, because you are passionate about the director. He makes you read a script and the script becomes the most important thing to you for a moment of your life. Sharpness and precision might be another universe in which you live for a few months of a year. So everything in art changes; there isn't really a rule.

The moment you say this is how you do things, you then realize you have to do the opposite on your next film.

Sun-Ryung KIM CGK

Cinematographer

My dream was to be a director and I went to the United States to study directing, but when I got involved in filmmaking I suddenly fell in love with cinematography and decided to be a cinematographer. I studied at the American Film Institute, where we shot on film and learned about film cameras, but when I came to Korea it was all changing to digital, so I am part of the in-between generation.

When I speak to film students I encourage them first to simply be a human and to learn how to create a story. I tell them that a camera is only a toy. If you have a great camera it does not come out with a great movie. It's always inside—you have to know how to be a storyteller and then the camera goes with the story. Studying cameras is good, but don't think of yourself just as a technician. Cinematography is also the ultimate artistic expression of human life. So, as a cinematographer, you need to have a profound understanding of life and you need to develop an artistic sense.

I also have to say that although a camera is just a thing, the ALEXA is kind of interactive; it gives an interactive feeling to things, almost like a conversation with the camera. You have to take from ALEXA, you have to learn, but it gives you a path to becoming a great cinematographer. So I feel it is a living thing. I've learned a lot from ALEXA.

I am part of the
in-between generation.

Bill Klages

Lighting Designer

My anniversary date in show business is November 1948, when I was hired by the National Broadcasting Company in New York City as a television engineer and, as a result, experienced the earliest days of television broadcast. After a few years on the technical side of the industry, my career was interrupted by a two-year tour of active duty in the US Navy. Upon my return to NBC, I found that the large expansion in TV's popularity and the need for more programming resulted in a welcome opportunity to became a lighting director. The first show I lit, with no prior experience, was a 90-minute live, prime-time network show in an 18,000 square-foot studio. I was 26 years old.

The ARRI 650 came at an interesting time. In television, lighting people discovered that they were over-lighting their sets, because we weren't paying much attention to camera development and as each new set of cameras came out, they became more sensitive. Along comes this ARRI 650–it was the perfect size and accommodated the update in the sensitivity of the camera.

Lighting at that time was a joy because of the independence.

The 650 had four-way barndoors, each door a fixed shape and size. On first using the instrument, I found that the vertical cut of the lamp was a little bit too high and the horizontal edges did not extend to the full width of the lamp, so I actually cut off part of the side doors with sheet metal snips. Then I went to ARRI and about a year or two later came the "Bill Klages" four-way, eight-leaf barndoor with adjustable sides for the ARRI 650.

Television lighting during most of my career was a joy because of the independence. Nobody was instructing me or telling me what to do. There was never a budgetary restraint, and I can't remember anyone ever saying, "If you can do it in 12 hours, can you not do it in 10?" Who has that freedom today? I'm talking about a golden age that maybe nobody will ever see again.

Igor Klebanov RGC

Cinematographer

I suppose that in our profession of cinematography, elements of art and technique have merged into one individuality. Of course, I give supremacy to the creative component. Equipment should serve me in comprehending and achieving the phenomenon of art—the art of visual metaphor.

My dealings with the four magical letters ARRI began in 1980. For the 1980 Olympics in Moscow, the Soviet Union obtained a large amount of ARRI camera equipment. Over the 35 years since then, those dealings have not let up!

This is first-class equipment that lets you not think about equipment. Amazing cameras with splendid ergonomics: when we slung it on our shoulders, it felt like a sweetheart curling up to you. It truly was an organic whole. Today's abundance of equipment helps cinematographers to make any vision of the director a reality.

> This is first-class equipment that lets you not think about equipment.

In ARRI's centennial year, as we bid farewell to film, we pay tribute to the great film alliances: Federico Fellini and Gianni di Venanzo; Ingmar Bergman and Sven Nykvist; Andrei Tarkovsky and Vadim Yusov; Andrzej Wajda and Jerzy Lipman; István Szabó and Lajos Koltai; and, of course, two great geniuses of world cinema: Mikhail Kalatozov and Sergey Urusevsky. We bow down to them!

Mikhail Krichman RGC

Cinematographer

The veil of magic that comes from film has only intensified with the process of its departure. I'm not prone to mystification: yes, there is chemistry here, and electricity there. Yes, you can hold analog, and not digital. If it hasn't been copied three times by the time the producer gets to the office—what's happened to it?

I have realized it's no good trying to pass one off as the other. After all the attempts and, not quite mistakes but tests, you realize that you are simply trying to pass off fantasy as reality. You are trying to make film out of digital. You're looking for the key to make it feel right: "Let's make it look like 5219, or 5247." That's the wrong tack. If you need 5219, then get 5219! Meanwhile, the upsides of digital need to be pulled out of it; you just need to learn to use digital so that it brings the same joy as film.

I'm quite used to depending on the camera like it's a soldier. Not because it's made of iron, but because it has rarely let me down, for the most part.

It seems to me that the perseverance and the continuity with which the people at ARRI create cameras and

I'm quite used to depending on the camera like it's a soldier.

instruments only demonstrates how much they love it. So in my view it would be vulgar to give them any advice. Well, perhaps the only thing is that I would like to continue framing through an optical viewfinder, not an LCD. I'd love for them to keep those cameras in service just a little while longer, so I can use my eye and get light through the lens right onto my retina. To watch through a viewfinder that creates space, with depth and definition, like you're used to seeing on the screen.

Danielle Krieger & Casey Warren

Director, Producer   Cinematographer, Director

We have been working together since we both started out with our own passions in the visual industry, and it's sort of like one brain; we approach things from different directions but we have the same aesthetic. Between us we cover the overall vision and also the infinite possibilities of little details, so when we come together it's like a full circle experience.

From 1994 was a very personal project that we made just for ourselves. We shot on the ALEXA M and we lit it with as much natural light as possible. One of our favorite scenes is the biking scene. We mounted the camera on the MōVI, on a go-cart, and we followed these kids on bikes. It was something that we wanted to get a lot of energy out of, rather than being static; we wanted to be with those kids—riding with them, swirling around them and doing all this cool stuff while they were on the bikes.

Casey actually drew sketches of what our perfect camera would be.

During the process of *From 1994* and then continuing to use the ALEXA M, we just wanted a smaller camera. Casey actually drew sketches of what our perfect camera would be. Then at NAB we met the guys from ARRI, showed them the sketches and they were like, "We are working on something that is pretty close to what you're hoping for." They started sending us renderings and we kept giving comments back. Eventually it evolved into the ALEXA Mini—an awesome little camera that you can take anywhere. You can put it on a gimbal, or on a drone, or you can throw it in your backpack on a hike.

Ellen Kuras ASC

Cinematographer, Director

Working with Martin Scorsese on a project for HBO, I was looking to create a triptych of moving video backgrounds of New York's city skyline. It would be a duration piece, so for some of the images we used time-lapse and for others, slow motion. MS had the idea of using the hand-crank camera he had received as a gift. He was enthusiastic: "Let's see if it actually works." So I called up Phil, our lens tech at ARRI in New York, and asked him to check it out. "It works!" Phil exclaimed, "And we were able to give it a thorough tech checkup, too!" He and the other ARRI techs made sure it was calibrated, so we went out to test it, wooden tripod legs and all.

Our perception changes, based on the technology.

In the old days, cinematographers used to sing a song to keep the camera at crank speed, so I contacted a cinematographer whose grandfather was one of the original members of the ASC and who had a huge collection of old hand-crank cameras. He helped me to set up the camera. I said, "So, now do we sing the song?" He laughed, "Oh, no, now you can get the timing on your iPhone." I chose for us to sing the song on that rooftop!

Looking at that footage, it was clear that there is a different way to perceive material that is shot on a hand-crank camera, at 18 frames per second. Our perception changes,

based on the technology, and that very much relates to today's digital world. A lot of us who started out in film have to readjust our way of looking at the new digital image. It can appear too sharp to us, too hyper-real. So we mess with it, use anamorphic lenses or take light off the background to give it more texture and depth. But when you look at the next generation, kids who go to film school are never going to use film cameras. They're only going to use digital cameras, and they accept what we think of as horrible, completely un-filmlike images. So it's really intriguing to see how the technology has changed our perception, how it actually changes culture.

Ed Lachman ASC

Cinematographer

The language of cinema is images, not words, and images are like music; they are a nonverbal form of communication.

The TV series *Mildred Pierce* takes place in the 1930s and we wanted to bring out the austereness of the time. On *Carol*, by Patricia Highsmith, we wanted to document still photographers like Helen Levitt, Esther Bubley and Ruth Orkin, who were experimenting with early color film. In both cases the director, Todd Haynes, and I felt we could capture the period through the grain of Super 16 mm.

My most recent film with Todd Haynes was *Wonderstruck*. Part of the film takes place in the 1920s, when we meet this young girl who is deaf. So about 40 percent of the film is in black-and-white, like a silent movie. Another part of the film takes place in the 1970s and that is in color, and then about 15 percent of it is digital, because we were shooting in the Natural History Museum and I couldn't use any lighting. So we married three aspects of film language. I didn't want the digital to be different than the filmic part, and I was pleasantly surprised. I was rating it at higher than EI 800 and I had really wonderful results.

I think digital media has its own look, the way film has its own look, and we should not worry that one has to be the other—we just embrace what it is. I like that we have options to tell our stories in different languages and we do not use one brush or one color to paint our pictures.

I think digital media has its own look, the way film has its own look.

A history told through stories

ARRI products are considered to be precise, robust and reliable, but the people behind the products have always been much more than engineers and tinkerers. The founders, August Arnold and Robert Richter, were cameramen who became manufacturers out of their love for visual storytelling. Today, this spirit still forms the cornerstone of the company: film enthusiasts developing tools for filmmakers. The close connection between designers and creative users is one of the secrets behind ARRI's success.

On the occasion of ARRI's 100th anniversary, we wanted to hear from cinematographers, directors, lighting technicians, inventors, historians and users. We reached out, and we were overwhelmed by the response—hundreds of people from every continent and every side of the industry came forward to be interviewed on camera. They spoke about their passion for telling stories, their love of film, their enthusiasm for technology and their individual experiences with ARRI. From these interviews, film editors around the world have created around 300 short films. You can watch them all at www.100.arri.com/filmmakersview

Given the scale of the project, revealed over the next few pages, this book could never really have painted a complete picture. Offered here are selected highlights from selected interviews, but we are truly grateful to each and every person who sat down to speak with us, and can only say, in thanks and in hope: to be continued ...

> Katja von Garnier
Director

> Ewa Karlström
Producer

> Sing-Pui O HKSC
Director, Producer

^ Cory Geryak
Cinematographer

> Cai Quanyong
Gaffer, Professor of BFA

> Willy Kurant AFC
Cinematographer

v Esther Gronenborn
Director

< Kang Xiaotian
Gaffer

v Hou Yong DP
Professor of Shanghai
Theatre Academy

< Lou Ye
Director

< Jim Baltazar
President & Managing Director
of CMB Film Services Inc.

> Wang Yu
Cinematographer

< Doo-Yong LEE
Director

> Alwin Küchler BSC
Cinematographer

v Arthur Cooper CSC
Cinematographer

v Kosuke Yamada JSC
Cinematographer

< Keiko Nakahara
Cinematographer

^ Won-Ki HONG
Director

^ Joon-Hong KIM
Cinematographer

> Hermann Krug
Advertising Producer

> Bert Dunk ASC
Cinematographer

> Julia von Heinz
Director

^ Christian Sebaldt ASC, BVK
Cinematographer

> Nicolai Mehring
Cinematographer

> Lv Yue
Cinematographer

< Franz Rath BVK
Cinematographer

> Yoshihito Kinoshita
CTO, Tokyo Laboratory LTD.

> Bozhena Maslennikova
Colorist

> Gerhard Fromm
Innovator

v Apurba Kishore Bir
Cinematographer

^ Mike Pandey
Director

< Anatoliy Petritskiy
Cinematographer

^ Robby Baumgartner
Cinematographer

< Alexandre Ilkhovski RGC
Cinematographer

v Maxim Trapo RGC
Cinematographer

< Carmen Treichl
Cinematographer

> Lin Wenjie
General Manager,
Starlight Films

^ Bella Halben
Cinematographer

< Vadim Alisov RGC
Cinematographer

< Xie Zhengyu
Cinematographer

> Maria Solovyeva RGC
Cinematographer

> Yuriy Klimenko
Cinematographer

^ Vladimir Klimov RGC
Cinematographer

< Du Jie
Cinematographer

^ "Nelson" Yu Likwai
Cinematographer

^ KK Senthil Kumar ISC
Cinematographer

> Feng Xiaogang
Director

> Mikhail Agranovich
Cinematographer

> Sergey Trofimov RGC
Cinematographer

> Kong Sheng
Director

> Igor Bogdasarov
Technical Director, Mosfilm

> Connie Walther
Director

> Paul Sarossy ASC, BSC, CSC
Cinematographer

> Hans Fischer
Cinematographer

v Guillaume Schiffman AFC
Cinematographer

v Julian Krubasik
Cinematographer

< Takeshi Hamada JSC
Cinematographer

^ Masakazu Ishii
Gaffer

< Douglas Trumbull
Director, Special Effects Innovator

> Tien-Jung Lin
Chairman, ARROW Cinematic Group Beijing

> Tien-Keui Lin
Chairman, ARROW Cinematic Group Taiwan
Producer

> Markus Nestroy
Cinematographer

< Fred Elmes ASC
Cinematographer

< Jean-Marie Dreujou AFC
Cinematographer

> Rob McLachlan ASC, CSC
Cinematographer

< Alvaro Brito
Gaffer

^ Preetha Jayaraman IWCC
Cinematographer

> Paul Yee
Cinematographer

^ Marie Noëlle
Director

> John Velez
Gaffer

^ Richard Ladkani
Cinematographer, Director

^ Walerio Rosa
Gaffer

^ Markus Förderer BVK
Cinematographer

^ Stefan Arndt
Producer, X Filme Creative Pool

^ Bill Holshevnikoff
Cinematographer

> Dagmar Hirtz
Director

^ Minoru Kawai JSL
Lighting Technician

> Hideki Mochizuki JSL
Gaffer

< Chang-Yun SUNG
Producer

> Jae-Young Lim
Gaffer

˅ Timo Salminen FSC
Cinematographer

< Lotta Killian BVK
Cinematographer

> Michael Apted
Director

˅ Mike Valentine BSC
Cinematographer

^ Jeff Allen
Managing Director,
Panavision UK

^ Christine A. Maier
Cinematographer

˅ Neil Harvey
Cinematographer

> Nicolette Krebitz
Director

˅ Mohamed Ashoub
Chairman, New Vision Media
& Film Systems

< Bebe Dierken BVK
Cinematographer

˅ Johann Perry
Cinematographer

^ Svetlana Cvetko
Cinematographer

> Marwan Hamed
Director

> He Quan
General Manager,
Cinerent Beijing Ltd.

˅ Christoph Krauss BVK
Cinematographer

^ Luciano Tovoli AIC, ASC
Cinematographer

< Eeva Fleig
Cinematographer

^ Shahram Aderangui
Cinematographer

< Zhang Huijun
Principal of BFA

> Wael Darwish
Cinematographer

˅ Martin Moszkowicz
CEO, Constantin Film

< Kitaro Kanematsu JSC
Cinematographer

> Sophie Darlington
Cinematographer

> Marieke Schroeder
Director

Ang Lee

Director

I read *Life of Pi*, Yann Martel's book, when it first came out. Philosophically it's a story examining the value of stories, and I didn't think you could do that in a film. Seven years later, *Life of Pi* sort of chose me. Fox 2000 had the rights available, but I hesitated for another year. Finally, I had the thought that if I had an additional dimension, a third dimension, maybe that would inspire me to find new approaches.

While I was making *Life of Pi*, I often wondered whether I would be the same filmmaker when I went back to 2D. I guess not, because my eyes are now 3D trained. I have a different pair of eyes.

The biggest thing I missed when I made the transition from film to digital was the chemical dots. They are not controllable; they seem to have a life of their own. I still miss a lot of the film aspects of cinema, but it is more cultural than technical, because film is something I grew up with; I miss my innocence, my childhood, what I used to believe. But it is important to embrace what you have and to find a new chemistry. This way, you can find a new art.

That was my journey making *Life of Pi* with digital cameras in 3D. I felt a lot like I was adrift on the Pacific, alone with the tiger; that was the process, but once you get to the other shore it is another story.

The clarity of digital images gave me an incentive to find something new and I don't want to feel intimidated by it, because we can never chase our imagination enough. We can never chase the technology enough, because it is God's work we are trying to imitate and we are still far from grasping it, so I will keep chasing. In the meantime, I do not want people to tell me that 24 fps is where you should stop. I want to have my own contribution, my own discoveries.

I felt a lot like I was adrift on the Pacific, alone with the tiger.

Matthew Libatique ASC

Cinematographer

When I was becoming interested in filmmaking as an undergrad, I did not study film; I was in sociology and communications—I had this idea that I wanted to make these little tiny movies about petty crimes. The one camera they had was an ARRIFLEX 16ST, and it had a variable speed motor in it. Once, this motor was set to reverse and when I got the footage back I had double exposed everything. I looked at it and I was just sort of inspired by the mistake, and on subsequent shootings I tried to keep producing it. I kept trying it over and over again because it was perfect when I did it by mistake, but when I was trying to repeat the findings it was just too scientific. I have always looked back on that moment and I kind of made a career out of those mistakes working out.

Complacency and comfort have nothing to do with our business.

Hopefully you are taking a film because there is something about it you really want to do. You do it for something that is going to keep you getting up at a godawful early call time or standing up for 16 hours; something has got to keep you going. I think films are really hard to make, and it takes a lot out of you, but complacency and comfort have nothing to do with our business.

You have got to go the extra mile in terms of trying to be inspired as a filmmaker or as an artist in general. Like the things you believe in, the things that move you, the things that make you click and the things that make you inspired or angry or happy, all those things should go into your content, or else you have nothing to shoot. You really have to go with kind of an abandon when you are trying to create something special.

Juliane Lorenz

President, Rainer Werner Fassbinder Foundation

Rainer Werner Fassbinder was not very much interested in his films once they were finished. But the TV series *Berlin Alexanderplatz* was his baby, from his early youth on, and he was very proud of it.

When the Fassbinder Foundation started to restore Fassbinder's TV films, we began with *Berlin Alexanderplatz*, which was shot on 16 mm in 1979/1980. We decided to scan the original negative, restore it digitally in 2K and then produce a new 35 mm negative of the restoration. At that time it was still a kind of pioneering experience to do digital restorations, but we had an amazing partner in ARRI, who had a background in analog films and was a pioneer in creating machines for digital film. That's how we got together: ARRI had just developed the ARRISCAN. There is no other scanner like it in the world.

Restoring a film is kind of rewriting a film. It's not only a question of how the film looked originally and how you transform that analog look into new digital data. There is also the question: What would Fassbinder have done? I am convinced he would have loved to experience this new process, and I insisted from the very beginning on including his original DPs in the restorations. So Michael Ballhaus was involved in the restoration of *World on a Wire* and Xaver Schwarzenberger in the case of *Berlin Alexanderplatz.* We all remembered what Rainer had once

Restoring a film is kind of rewriting a film.

had in mind for the color grading, but now it had to be transferred into a digital grading process. So we and the ARRI restoration team checked the screening material resources: the faded 16 mm prints and a Beta SP transfer of an original magnetic tape transfer of the screening print, made in the early 1970s. Although these materials were faded, it was helpful to double-check the final look.

We do not know yet if you can keep the flame of original linear films that have been restored digitally for all eternity, but as we created new 35 mm negatives of the restorations with the ARRILASER—as well as keeping the original materials in good condition—there will always be proof of their original beauty. And at least there is the hope that these analog restored safety negatives will survive longer than all the digital data, which probably will not last forever.

Hans Albrecht Lusznat BVK

Cinematographer

The history of the ARRIFLEX 35BL is connected to the history of sound. Working with the original sound requires a silent camera. The idea was to mount the sprockets, the movement, and everything else that produced noise on one single unit, to isolate it from the camera body. So the sprockets and the film gate float on rubber, without any contact to the housing. The ARRIFLEX 35BL was an ingenious solution. You could operate it on your shoulder, and changing a magazine was pretty fast. The viewfinder rotated by up to 180 degrees and the image always stayed level.

I bought this camera because it is a beautiful object.

The first film shot on a 35BL was *Across 110th Street* (1972), which was filmed on location in Harlem and tells the story of a bank robbery. They used a handheld style and moved the camera lot. The film was a low-budget production, but it introduced a whole new look and style.

In 1973, Joachim Gerb and Erich Kästner of ARRI won a Scientific and Engineering Award for their work on the ARRIFLEX 35BL. I bought this camera because it is a beautiful object. There is very little equipment that is so well made—where form and function complement each other so perfectly. This camera exudes its own beauty.

Sophie Maintigneux

Cinematographer

In 1976 I did an internship on Coline Serreau's first film, *Pourquoi Pas!* At the time, I actually wanted to become an actress, but one day I was alone on set and saw the ARRIFLEX 35BL camera standing on a tripod, and I just had to walk over to it. I'd seen how the camera assistant always opened a little hatch on the side to change the film magazines, and I really wanted to see what the camera looked like on the inside.

I can still remember just how apprehensive I was when I opened the hatch. It was almost a magical moment. Of course, the camera assistant came running up to me in an agitated state and scolded me terribly: What did I think I was doing? Now the film was exposed and ruined. I was mortified, but luckily everything was okay. Today, I'm happy that my dream of a career in front of the camera didn't materialize, and that I stayed on the other side, as one of those people who is allowed to open the little hatch on the side of the camera.

I really wanted to see what the camera looked like on the inside.

Hank McElwee

Executive in Charge of Cinematography, NFL Films

A typical week for me starts on a Saturday, getting on an airplane, flying to a football game, shooting the game on Sunday and flying back home Sunday night. Back in the film days I always dreaded Monday, when I check footage from all the different games, because sometimes our film was x-rayed before it got on the airplane and came back ruined. Tuesday I'm out finding crew for the 54 cameras we use each week at different stadiums; Wednesday and Thursday I spend color grading; and on Friday I try to relax.

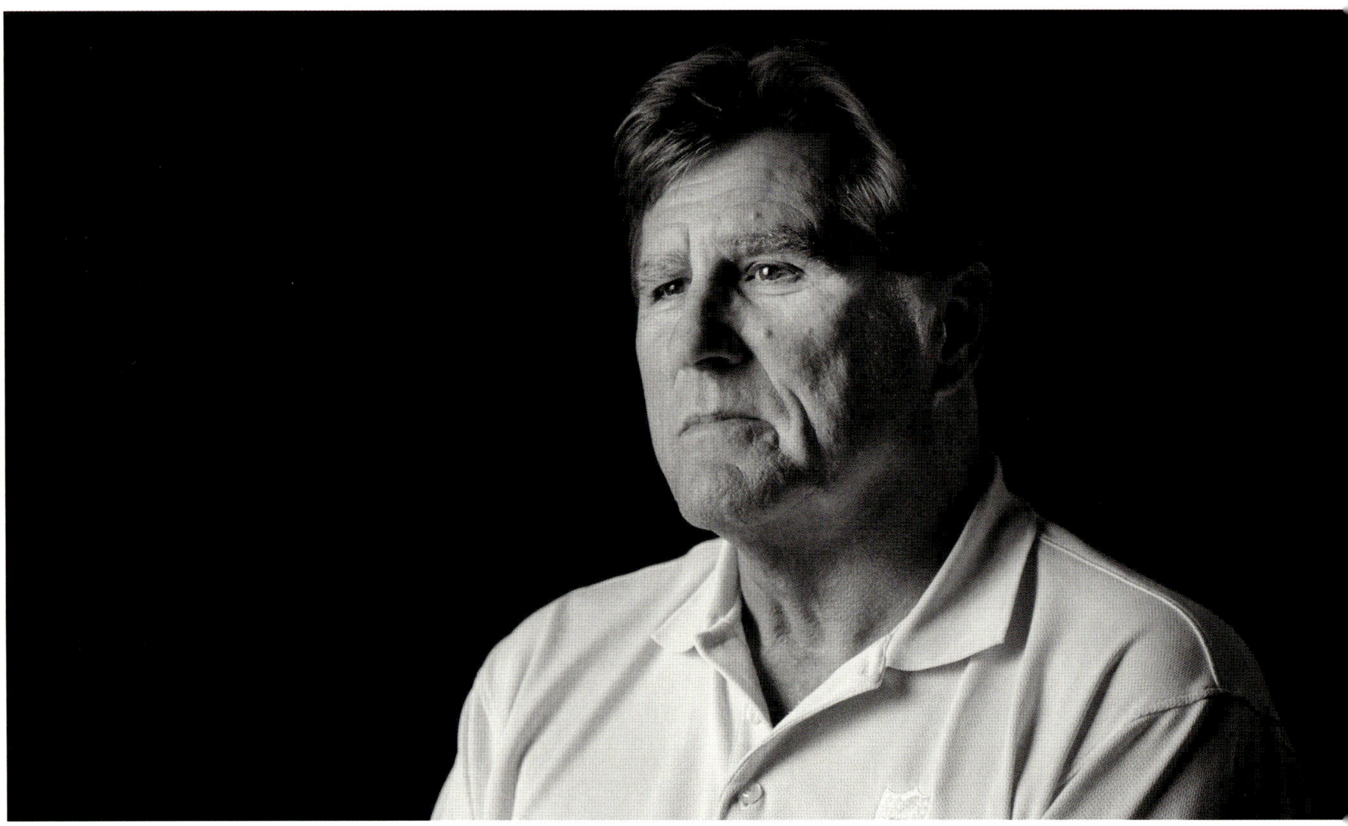

In the National Football League film library we have 110 million feet of film, which equates to 19,000 miles. It was March 2014 when our CFO told us that we were no longer going to shoot on film. We had three months to make the transition to digital because one of our major shows wanted to air on Tuesday nights and there was no way we could have got everything done on time using film.

I looked at a lot of different manufacturers' cameras. The most important thing to me was the eyepiece; we have to be able to follow the ball in the air. Sport cinematography is all about seeing what you're shooting, and the ARRI AMIRA was amazing for that. In July 2013 I got my first 30 cameras and that was probably the best year my cinematographers ever had. It made everybody better.

You have no idea how much fun it is to be out there on Sundays shooting professional football.

I am now 67 years old and I'm still shooting football. You have no idea how much fun it is to be out there on Sundays shooting professional football, especially when you have great games. There's nothing like it; I wouldn't give it up for anything.

Chris Menges BSC, ASC

Cinematographer

Our job is simply to serve the story, to catch words and performances, so whenever possible I have always operated the camera. While I'm doing a shot, I can see what coverage is needed; I can check the lighting and the ratios, and sense the feeling and the atmosphere. It totally concentrates the mind. You see things on the ground glass that you can never see on the monitor, so it's the operator who knows what's going down.

I operated for Brian Probyn on Ken Loach's first film, *Poor Cow*, and that was an ARRIFLEX 35 IIC in a blimp. It was the same setup when I operated for Miroslav Ondříček on Lindsay Anderson's *If....*, and again when I shot my first feature film in 1969, which was *Kes* for Ken Loach. So, you could say that my roots are in the IIC.

My ambition had always been to go out at night and shoot the sky, and see it.

In 2010, Stephen Daldry asked me to serve as the director of photography on *Extremely Loud & Incredibly Close*. Stephen and I were open to shooting on film or digital; we did various tests with ALEXA and ended up being the first feature film to record ARRIRAW. My ambition had always been to go out at night and shoot the sky, and see it. To do that on film is obviously quite hard, but the ALEXA could do it easily, and to me that was a major breakthrough.

With film you always wake up in the middle of the night thinking, "I've blown it, haven't I?" And you don't know how it went until the next day, or if you're on location overseas, maybe two or three months. But the thing about shooting digitally is: what you've got, you see. You can, in a funny way, be braver. You can take risks that perhaps you wouldn't dare to on film, unless you're a bit crazy.

Reed Morano ASC

Cinematographer, Director

I resisted moving from film to digital for a long time. It was very depressing for me when everyone was saying film is dead, but when the ALEXA came out it really was a turning point. It looked worlds above any other digital camera. I was intrigued and encouraged by it, but I still couldn't shake my love for film. Maybe it's the inherent nostalgia, maybe it's the texture, but I actually think for me it's an emotional thing. And ALEXA was the first camera that created imagery that didn't hamper my emotions.

There's a learning curve choosing lenses and lighting coming from film, which is so forgiving. Lighting for digital is a different process for me, in order to give it texture and emotion. It took me probably until I shot *Meadowland* to really be happy with how digital looked in my hands.

> You truly become another character in the scene when you're holding the camera.

On both *Meadowland* and my latest film I directed, *I Think We're Alone Now*, I shot ALEXA and I was the DP and I also operated, because it's such an intimate story. As the director, that's a huge luxury. There were moments where I was holding the camera and I would reach out and I could touch the actors or whisper to them, and that affected the performance. Every operator will agree that you truly become another character in the scene when you're holding the camera. Every move I make is a reaction to what the actor does. It's most exciting when I don't know where I might go next with the camera.

Digital is its own animal and I had to transform to adapt to it, but that's how I learn. I can tell my stories on film if I want to, or I can shoot ALEXA, and either way I'm going to be able to elicit real emotions from the audience, which is the most important thing for me as a storyteller.

Kramer Morgenthau ASC

Cinematographer

The transition from film to digital was rough in the beginning and then kind of settled down once the ALEXA came out. I feel like it standardized things, and everybody understood it. You could just forget about the camera again and do what you were originally supposed to be doing: telling a story visually with light, with color, with texture, with movement.

When I first started working with ALEXA and stopped using film, I wouldn't really say I lit differently; I still pushed hard on shadow and light, and the camera captured it all beautifully. Today, I'd say that I probably do light differently for digital, but I also feel like styles have changed.

I recently did a project called *Rebel in the Rye*, which is a J. D. Salinger biopic. I worked with spherical lenses that were quite fast, and really low light levels. It was a smaller budget film, so I chose a smaller footprint approach to filmmaking—using a lot of available light and also using the ARRI SkyPanels with a piece of software called Luminair, which controls them wirelessly. I could sit at a monitor with an iPad and my gaffer, and we could literally paint with light. You can react to the monitor and the actors, and change light levels during the shot. It was a different style that came out of necessity, but a really nice use of technology to be more creative, which is what it should be all about.

Sometimes the smaller pictures are more liberating creatively because the machine is smaller; it's more intimate and the stakes aren't as high. There is less fear and more expression, versus worrying about this giant net that you're dragging behind you wherever you go.

I could sit at a monitor with an iPad and my gaffer, and we could literally paint with light.

Rachel Morrison ASC

Cinematographer

Since I was six or seven, I always had a camera in my hand. I feel incredibly fortunate to have discovered a passion for photography at such a young age. Ultimately, the decision I had to make was whether to become a photojournalist or a cinematographer, and I decided that I preferred the collaborative nature of film.

I think the nonfiction work I did early on helped to shape who I am as an operator, as well as my appreciation for natural light. Learning how to instinctually dance with the camera in response to somebody else's emotion is a strangely specific skill set; I developed the ability to read the character that I was shooting. What I've come to realize is that in so many ways filmmaking is as much psychology as it is art.

What I've come to realize is that in so many ways filmmaking is as much psychology as it is art.

Mudbound is the story of the American dream, set in the deeply racist South of the 1940s. I've always been inspired by the Farm Security Administration photographers such as Gordon Parks, Dorothea Lange, Arthur Rothstein, Ben Shahn, Walker Evans and so many more. I saw this as my chance to honor them. It's actually one of the first period films I've shot, and it's truly a gift to be able to point your camera at what feels like a different time and place.

It felt almost sacrilegious not to shoot on film, but it just wasn't in the budget, so we wound up shooting digitally. ALEXA was a no-brainer for me because there's a humanity to the rendition of skin tones that no other digital camera seems to produce. We were shooting in tiny plantation homes from the late 19th century and every inch counted, so the ALEXA Mini was the perfect tool. Fortunately, the Mini had just gotten the Open Gate and the raw update, so we were able to shoot a mixture of anamorphic and spherical on ARRIRAW. In the end, I'm very happy with the way it looks.

I was the one who stayed up until midnight and took all those cameras apart.

Otto Nemenz

CEO, Otto Nemenz International, Inc.

Actually, it was at Panavision in 1964 that I saw an ARRI camera for the first time. It was an ARRIFLEX 35 IIC–Panavision had a lot of IIC cameras, and that was also the first camera I bought for myself.

At that time I was a camera assistant. I knew how to take a IIC apart and put it back together. When we were shooting on car commercials and a lot of dust and dirt got into the cameras, I was the one who stayed up until midnight and took all those cameras apart, cleaning them and getting them ready for the next day.

I always liked to own my own equipment, because the existing rental companies were not that good and their equipment wasn't in great shape. That got me to the point where I said, "I can do better." I started acquiring more equipment and founded my own rental company.

A lot of cameramen need something special; they come to us and say they want to do a shot where they hang the camera up or roll it down a stairway, and that's where we come in. With our ideas, our machine shop and our 3D printers, we can build equipment and accessories that didn't exist, and give them exactly what they want. Every time it is something different.

Nikolay Nemolyaev

Cinematographer

I shot *Assassin of the Tsar* with an ARRIFLEX 35BL 4 camera and it had a magnificent viewfinder. I constantly used filters and was able to give directions, make corrections and see exactly what the outcome would be.

There was one scene that required an extremely lengthy handheld shot. Malcolm McDowell, who played Yurovsky, walked down a staircase and along a corridor about 30 meters long, built on a set at Mosfilm. There were rooms off to the sides, and when he made it to the furthest room, he had a dialogue with another actor. While they said their lines, I turned the other way. Meanwhile, the electricians rearranged the lighting and I moved back to peer into the first, second and third rooms. The entire shot took up 150 meters of film. We were shooting with a 300-meter magazine, on a 24-kilogram camera, with counterweights. There were about four takes for the Russian version and another four takes for the English version. Going through eight times with all that weight was not easy, but the BL 4 was brilliantly balanced. When I walked, it felt like a Steadicam: nothing could shake it. The heavier the weight, the more stable it was, and the smoother the image.

Of the paints used by Vermeer, Salvador Dalí once said, "I could do with some like that..." The materials and tools an artist uses, like the cameras and lenses a cinematographer uses, are very important. I am grateful to ARRI equipment for the opportunities I was given and took advantage of in my work.

The materials and tools an artist uses, like the cameras and lenses a cinematographer uses, are very important.

Zeng Nianping

Cinematographer, Director, Guest Lecturer at BFA

During my time at Beijing Film Academy I watched a lot of Chinese films, and I noticed a drastic difference between Chinese films and foreign films. Foreign films were more naturally lit, while Chinese films had very artificial lighting due to technical limitations. The fake and artificial lighting was obnoxious to me, so I was determined to change that.

The film *Blush* was the first time I extensively used ARRI lights, and it totally unleashed my creativity. The story was about a group of sex workers in a rehabilitation facility shortly after China's liberation.

At that time, most Chinese films did not have a sufficient budget and had to use Chinese-made lights with inconsistent color temperature. They did not last very long and would require constant lamp replacement, which caused many issues. ARRI lights made the entire workflow a lot easier. We also recorded sync sound for the film because the ARRIFLEX 35BL 4 camera allowed us to do that. Later the movie was submitted to the Berlin International Film Festival. It was surprisingly well received, and the whole team won a Silver Bear for visual shaping.

My theory is that filmmaking technologies and tools have been pushing the art. Science and technology are the foundation of the art of filmmaking. In turn, the art of filmmaking keeps driving the science and technology forward. It is a symbiotic relationship, and I think ARRI has played an important role in the process.

Science and technology
are the foundation
of the art of filmmaking.

Sean O'Neill

Gaffer

In my early years there weren't many big international productions coming to New Zealand, so I grew up working on low-budget local films with small crews. I worked for some very good gaffers and I learned my craft from these guys. One of them was Don Jowsey; we worked together on the Jane Campion films *An Angel at My Table* and *The Piano*, and then in 1996 we went to London to do *The Portrait of a Lady*. I was the best boy on the film, and Don was the gaffer.

In New Zealand at the time we did not have the culture of the big rental company. So in 1999 I decided to buy my own equipment and I started with ARRI equipment. It had filtered down from Europe and we knew it to be reliable and well engineered, so I started that long relationship and it still exists today.

As an owner-operator you are very much more conscious about looking after the gear, so I've still got all the items —still working—20 years later.

I decided to buy my own equipment and I started with ARRI equipment.

Of course I've bought more and more equipment, it never stops, and now we are at the gateway of new technologies with LED. It's an exciting time.

We've got these incredible tools being made available to us, in terms of output, in terms of usability—we're saving energy, we're saving man-hours—and they are simplifying our job, giving us more options. In the old days we would do a big studio set and put up 150 space lights, and run tons of copper cable to six generators in the car park. We don't need to do that anymore. When we needed to change the color of those lights we'd spend $5,000 on gel; now we just press a button on our computer and it's done. Our toolbox is ever expanding and everything has got its place, from the oldest lights to the newest technology.

I have learned that technical innovations can lead to a more diverse form of artistic expression.

Luo Pan

Cinematographer

Many people think wide-angle lenses have to be used for wide shots only. While watching the demo film of the ARRI Ultra Wide Zoom at the Shanghai International Film Festival, I came up with the idea of shooting an entire short film with this extreme wide-angle lens.

Since I am a Chinese cinematographer, I wanted to show something typically Chinese, and a bamboo forest seemed the perfect location. I had envisioned a sunny look, but on the day of shooting it was raining and really foggy as well. We couldn't wait for the rain to stop, so I decided to go ahead.

The look was unique. I watched the rain running down the bamboo and lingering at the joints, and was able to move the lens in very close. Another mesmerizing image was a wide shot of a man standing with his back to the camera. I just told him to stand still and to look into the sun appearing after the rain. The camera then pushes in to a close-up of a drop of sweat on his neck. I love that shot.

It fascinated me how the UWZ lens inspired me to a new approach—to do something unconventional. I have learned that technical innovations can lead to a more diverse form of artistic expression. I always wanted to do something different from the films others made, so this was a great experiment for me.

Roman Polanski

Director

I have been very lucky to work with the best DPs—I've learned a tremendous amount from them. I think ARRI is a great company, truly, so many movies, such a great history. On many films I have used ARRI cameras; my last film was shot with digital ARRI cameras. Digital gives you incredible possibilities. Now you can really do anything that comes through your head. You don't have to stop every 10 minutes to reload—the best moments are always while they are reloading—and you don't get scratches. I was always waiting for new inventions, new improvements.

I think what attracts people to theaters is not that they can have a bigger screen and better sound, it's the experience of watching an event surrounded by an anonymous audience.

I like depth of focus. I think the depth of focus should be infinite. Occasionally I try to go to longer lenses and get a little bit less depth behind the actors, but I'm never satisfied with it. When you change lenses, the differences between the shots can be shocking. In order to get a consistent image, sometimes I only use one or two lenses. I also shoot mainly with one camera because I simply believe that there is only one best angle. But once you start cutting it together, very often you discover that you were wrong.

Editing is essential. You do your best shooting, you are sure that a certain angle is the one that you really want and you

cannot imagine that there's another solution for it. You shoot a scene in some kind of master shot and only for safety you cover it with closer shots or some other angles. And very often in editing you think, "Oh, I was really clever to do those other shots because now I see that I must use some of them." But you don't know it until you really put it in the film.

Overwhelming the spectator is the current tendency, but I think what attracts people to theaters is not that they can have a bigger screen and better sound, it's the experience of watching an event surrounded by an anonymous audience. That is very human. People have always wanted it, whether it was a Greek theater or a Roman circus. When you watch a football match on television you see every detail of it and they replay important moments, yet people kill themselves to get a ticket to the real match in the stadium. It's similar to cinema: It's much better to see a good film in a packed theater than in your own bedroom.

Dick Pope BSC

Cinematographer

The camera we used on the first films I worked on as a clapper loader (2nd AC) in the late 1960s was this enormous machine, which was basically the small ARRIFLEX 35 IIC inserted into a huge blimp. When the ARRIFLEX 35BL came out it resulted in a revolution that changed everything in terms of feature filmmaking for anybody who was shooting in a modern guerrilla style, getting out of the studio into the real world.

Naked was my second film with Mike Leigh, all on location, and I did a lot of handheld on it, so the 35BL was perfect. One sequence near the end took place in a tiny bathroom and the only place we could get a position for about half the scene was in the toilet. The camera was sunk down there in the bowl itself, with me wedged behind it and Mike Leigh on the other side. The 35BL was just a great location camera and served me very well for quite a few years.

We found that Turner used yellow in his highlights and a blue-green teal in the shadow areas.

Trying to devise a look for *Mr. Turner* involved studying Turner's work and thinking about how to give the film this painterly, Turner-ish feel, especially in terms of the color palette that we used. We were never trying to copy his paintings on screen, rather evoking the world that he viewed and was surrounded by, thereby imbuing the film's look with that same mood. We found that Turner used

yellow in his highlights and a blue-green teal in the shadow areas; they give his paintings a slightly hyper feel and he used it extensively. So in our tests we added this teal into the shadow areas, and added this yellow into the highlights, but without affecting the skin tones. My biggest fear about shooting *Mr. Turner* digitally was that the skies would not be resolved as well as they would be on film. That didn't happen. The skies were perfectly rendered—as good as on film and, dare I say it, sometimes even better. Everything we did was aided invaluably by the ARRIRAW.

Norris Pope

Author

The ARRIFLEX 35 was the kind of camera you wanted for situations where you need to be very mobile and you cannot take a big studio camera. What was wonderful was that you still got images of theatrical quality.

During World War II, the ARRIFLEX was widely used by German combat cameramen. There were stories among Allied cameramen about what a terrific camera it was, and they were captured as German soldiers were captured—or sometimes presumably cameramen were killed. So the first ARRIFLEX cameras to enter North America had been used in the war.

Initially the ARRIFLEX was viewed as a newsreel or documentary camera, and it was frowned upon by the studio brass with their Mitchells, saying, "How can you shoot a feature film on this tiny little camera?" But over time people began using it for special shots in feature films and television.

One classic example is the high-speed muscle car chase through the hilly streets of San Francisco in *Bullitt*, with Steve McQueen. Peter Yates, the director of the film, and his DP, William A. Fraker, had decided that they were not going to under-crank, so the cars were really going that fast. They wanted to shoot it on location, and this would have been totally impossible without the ARRIFLEX. They actually wrecked one: it was behind a parked car and as the stuntman skidded around a corner he crashed into the car, which crashed into the camera and smashed it to bits. According to the director you could still see that in the shot, if you looked closely.

Initially the ARRIFLEX was viewed as a newsreel or documentary camera.

Another example is the chase sequence in *The French Connection*. When Gene Hackman was driving himself, they often had three cameras attached to the car: one over the seat, one pointed up at him and another in the front of the car. That is a superb sequence, and it owes everything to ARRIFLEX cameras.

And then there's *Easy Rider*, the countercultural tour de force that made the ARRIFLEX an unquestionably hip camera to use!

Davide Pozzi

Director, Cineteca di Bologna

The magic moment of a restoration process is when you open the can, because that is the moment you can touch the film. You have a dialogue with the film itself; it is something very emotional.

We are using the latest technology, but ultimately our job is a cross-point between technology and something really

artisanal, because we work with our hands. That is the secret of our job. One of the dangers of digital technology is that you can do everything—my job is to understand when we need to stop.

The day I had in my hands *The Arrival of a Train at La Ciotat Station* (1895) was maybe the best day of my life, because I was holding a piece of history. The Lumière brothers were very good photographers. Some of the early films are in really good shape, much better than certain color films from the 1980s. And we are talking about film stock that is now more than 120 years old—it's even older than ARRI!

Our job is a cross-point between technology and something really artisanal.

We also did the restoration of the very first Charlie Chaplin films. In 1914, Chaplin did some Keystone films; there are a little bit more than 30 films, and we were able to work on them.

My feeling is that film stock will always be available. I can bet that Kodak will never close. Today, people understand how important it is to preserve images for the future, and the safest way to preserve images is to go back again on film.

Helmut Prein

Gaffer

The best lighting approach is whatever supports the story at that very moment. Personally, I like to light a room rather than light actors, creating a mood to the location and then getting the actors in to see what they do. Giving the director and the actors the freedom to walk around as much as they want to and then, once they have blocked out the scene and the camera movement, just finalize the actors' key lights. That's my ideal working process.

On my first films, only the cameraman or operator would actually know what the image was like—what the frame lines were, what you got in the shot and what you didn't get. Later you had a tiny black-and-white monitor on the Moviecams, but still it was that miracle of looking through the viewfinder to see the real image, and nobody could really judge what the result was going to be until you saw the final result a couple of days later, when screening the rushes.

The best lighting approach is whatever supports the story at that very moment.

Video assists got better and better until we started shooting digital, and suddenly there are high definition monitors on the set and people think, "This is what it's going to look like," but it's not really what you will see on the big screen. In postproduction they will process it, dial in color tones and contrast; they might play around with power windows and add some other magic to it. I am always kind of astonished, watching the final result projected on screen.

Cinematography nowadays is still a creative process; instead of just watching the monitors I try to use my eyes and my imagination for inspiration as much as possible.

Rodrigo Prieto ASC, AMC

Cinematographer, Director

I just love cameras. As a camera apprentice it was very special to me, really it was magical, the whole thing of putting the camera together and oiling it, and the blimp for the lens because it was noisy. The camera itself was not, it was an ARRIFLEX 35BL 2, but when we used the zoom we had to put a blimp on it for the sound. Loading the film, finding the sprocket and where to put it in, there is a magical quality to that where you still had to kind of feel it, with no light or in a changing bag. That process was just thrilling—very tactile and sensorial. I remember loving the smell of the camera gear when I went into the camera truck, the oil and also the emulsion, there is a certain smell to that.

I really think that I found the best job in the world.

One thing that I really enjoy is when a film camera is rolling—its vibration and that sound; when you are close to the camera, operating it, and you have that little sound. It's like, okay, this is happening right now and it adds an importance to the moment—film is rolling and every frame is precious.

I really think that I found the best job in the world. I love it, and there is never a dull moment; there's always something happening and there's always a challenge, but also simply the gear is something I like. Even though I am not an expert in cameras—and in that sense I am very grateful for the great camera systems I have worked with throughout

the years—but I just love cameras and touching them. That is one of the reasons I have always enjoyed operating, just being close to the camera, it makes me feel like I am making a movie.

Edgar Reitz

Director

Where is uncharted territory? Many filmmakers, adventurers, and others plagued with wanderlust search their entire lives for the unknown abroad. However, traveling to foreign lands is not always a prerequisite for making discoveries. Sometimes one can sniff out the unknown close to home. In my film *Home from Home*, I offered Werner Herzog a small role playing the naturalist Alexander von Humboldt. In the summer of 2012, Werner came to visit me in the Hunsrück region of Germany to see the village of Schabbach, the setting of my *Heimat Trilogy*. I told him that this village doesn't exist. Schabbach is fictional. Even the family around which the story revolves, and even this Hunsrück and its history do not exist outside the film. They are just as fictional as the steamship that was pulled through the jungle and over the top of a mountain in *Fitzcarraldo*. Through Werner's involvement in *Home from Home* we come full circle. He who tries to find his fortune far afield, discovers that another soldier of fortune, someone like me, has searched for his happiness "at home." However, the concept of home, like the fabled El Dorado, exists only in fantasy; it's a narrative.

The point is always to capture dreams on film, to translate feelings into pictures.

In my 30-plus years of continuous work on *Heimat*, I have often been seen as someone who has found his inspiration in the Hunsrück and has continued to film his life and

personal experiences there. However, the opposite is true: I choose, of all places, my childhood home in order to search for the stories and images that only exist in the fantasy, the fear, the memories and the desires of someone who has left, someone who fled the nest. I still think it's a miracle that we are able to capture such emotions with a film camera. In this respect, making films is my dream profession. I have often said: "One makes films with one's eyes closed." (Kubrick describes it as "eyes wide shut.")

The point is always to capture dreams on film, to translate feelings into pictures, and it should always be the immaterial images that are brought to the screen.

Film is also a time machine. When we watch classic films or early movies, we are confronted with people who have long since passed away—the dead who still move us to tears or laughter! Where else does something like that exist? Humanity has never experienced the kind of physical effect actors have on audiences long after their death. Us film folk, with our art, have outwitted mortality! With film, we have found a medium in which time can be preserved and passed on.

Through the process of making film, the question of how our memory works has become the central topic of my life. In the days of covered wagons, for example, when there were no films, I can't imagine how people remembered. Did this concrete way of looking back at our visible, active world, which we take for granted today, even exist? At that time, people only possessed what they could see with closed eyes or describe with words.

Cinema has become mankind's collective remembrance medium, and the individual films are elements of humanity's worldview. In the future, it will be through film that we learn to see the world.

Ben Richardson

Cinematographer

The thing that I am always looking for in a script is when the strongest scenes are born out of the most profound feelings of the characters, or decisions they have to make. As a cameraman, the script for *Beasts of the Southern Wild* was my absolute dream of what a film could be. Above all, it carried two subjects that I have always been interested in: a kind of fantastical and surrealist study of the world, and a grounded, naturalistic portrait of people—in this case a little girl named Hushpuppy and her father, living on the edge of the Louisiana bayou.

We shot *Beasts* on Super 16 and it was an instinctive first choice. We were taking these cameras deep into the swamps and working with nonprofessional actors, so there was very little opportunity for retakes. The ARRIFLEX 416 is—to this day—my favorite piece of technology in the world, with its 11-minute run time and absolutely bomb-proof construction. It was just the right thing to have by our side.

My favorite part of moviemaking is when you can strip the technology away and make it all about just a point of view.

My favorite part of moviemaking is when you can strip the technology away and make it all about just a point of view. There is a scene pretty much at the beginning of the movie where Hushpuppy runs towards the camera with sparklers in her hands; that entire shot was accomplished by me hanging out the back of the producer's car as we drove across this bumpy, grassy terrain with not a light as far as we could see. When the sparklers went out we were all plunged back into pitch darkness, and I remember watching our little DVCAM playback of this grainy video tap, and just feeling like there was something truly special in that moment we had captured.

Gernot Roll BVK

Cinematographer

I'm not a cineaste. Black-and-white is just a way of telling a story, no more. But if you're going to film in black-and-white, then it must be black-and-white. Therefore, I always try to achieve the highest degree of contrast that is still watchable.

We filmed Edgar Reitz's *Home from Home* digitally and viewed the results right there on location, in black-and-white. But it isn't enough to simply take out the color signal. You need to have the black-and-white picture in mind from the beginning and generate the necessary contrast through the positioning of subjects against backgrounds, and through lighting.

Shooting digital makes you bolder.

Digital images have been criticized for a long time, and to some extent, they still are today. You always hear: "I want to see the film. I want to see the grain." Ironically, filmmakers have been trying to reduce the grain for over 100 years. Today, some people don't like the fact that it's no longer there, but I'm happy it's gone; I don't need it. I like to sit right at the front at the cinema, and I enjoy the lovely, clear pictures.

Shooting digital makes you bolder. With film, there was always that certain insecurity, before the rushes, that you'd messed up somewhere. When I filmed *Henri 4* on the

ARRIFLEX D-21 with Jo Baier, we sometimes sat in front of the monitor and added things—more daring lighting, more daring contrasts—that I would never have dared to try with film. If I'd been working with film, I would have built in some security measures, like adding more light or opening the aperture a bit wider. After that experience we said, "No more film. Never again." And I've never worked with film again.

I want to keep in my mind more than a century of film history.

Yoichi Sai

Director

Life is not exactly sweetness and light the whole time; there are bright and dark moments, stillness and change. Life is an eternal up and down, and that's the reason why there are dramas.

The science of the 20th century created this art form called film. It transcended national identities and became a worldwide phenomenon. Like human life, film consists of light and shadows. For over 120 years, analog film was an important part of our experience and eventually it will disappear. For me as a director, the challenge is to link analog film with modern technology.

These days, you can develop analog film only in Osaka, which is 500 kilometers away from Tokyo. Fuji stopped producing film stock, which has necessitated the transition from analog to digital. I am thinking about shooting my next film with the ALEXA, but even if I use a digital camera I wish to pay tribute to film. I want to keep in my mind more than a century of film history. I want to preserve the atmosphere of analog film.

Roberto Schaefer ASC, AIC

Cinematographer

For me, good cinematography is based on composition and lighting, framing and camera movement—using the images to push the story forward, when it's a narrative. But there is also great cinematography that is non-narrative, that's just about making images that speak to different people in different ways.

On every job I go through that dilemma of what is the right lens to use for this show—is it the softness of a vintage lens, and then if you use real vintage lenses will they last through the production? Are they robust enough—are there replacements available if you need them? Or is there something being made now that emulates the vintage look? The Master Prime lenses do have their own texture, but they bring a purity to the image. I like the fact that you can capture reality, in a sense, although I use filters—I almost never shoot them clean. There's something about those lenses that is very pleasing.

So many people working today have never shot on film; they have only worked with digital and they have such a different concept of lighting and exposure, and of how to work with the material. I really think it's a disadvantage. If you know the basics of how lighting and exposure works, and where you can go with it, then it's a great help to being more creative.

So many people working today have never shot on film.

Volker Schlöndorff

Director

As a director, you have to be able to give the cameraman a feeling for the actors. But some cameramen seem to already have it in them, and you don't have to say a word. For example Sven Nykvist always knew exactly what was going on with an actor. He even filmed if there was still a tripod or a lamp in the background; he couldn't have cared less, so long as he was able to capture the moment when the actor was ready and at his most expressive.

A cameraman needs to understand that the actor is the most important person on set. Changing the light between two takes is fatal; it throws him off completely. You dare not break his concentration on the role he's playing. Instead, you need to help him to give of his best, and a digital camera is the optimum tool for that. With Stellan Skarsgård in *Return To Montauk*, we filmed three, four, five takes, one after the other, without putting the camera down. We simply went back to the beginning again and again. And mostly without someone calling out "action," so that we didn't lose the thread. Previously, we couldn't afford to do that. Every meter of film cost money, and sometimes I even screamed at the clapperboard operators if they were too slow, because by the time they'd got their act together, another meter of film had run through the camera.

A cameraman needs to understand that the actor is the most important person on set.

Today, we can run through a scene as often as we want, to the benefit of the work and the actors. Because of the repetition, a natural relationship develops between the camera and the actor. He becomes more and more relaxed, and at some point he forgets the moment when someone shouts, "Action! Now jump into the water." He's already in the water. He's swimming and we're swimming with him.

Nancy Schreiber ASC

Cinematographer

I was the fourth woman to join the ASC—and what an unbelievable honor. To be accepted, I had to show my work to many of my idols. Some of the "old-timers" had never seen any women in technical departments on set, let alone women cinematographers. I was a nervous wreck. I remember climbing what seemed like an endless staircase into the ASC clubhouse that day. Some years later I noticed there are only two steps to the porch landing. It certainly was a metaphor for my long climb up the ladder.

There's no reason that cinematography has to be gender-based, even though traditionally it was a man's job. The term cameraman is still used to this day, and I have been called a woman cameraman.

Unfortunately I never met the first woman admitted into the ASC, Brianne Murphy. I saw her interviewed, saying that people thought her name was Brian when checking her availability. She certainly surprised people when she showed up for work. Brianne was the only one at that time, working in Hollywood. As the decades passed, the numbers of women DPs slowly increased, and I do mean slowly. I feel, however, that the younger women and people of color coming up today will do better—and are already doing better—than my generation did, in terms of breaking through into the larger productions.

There's no reason that cinematography has to be gender-based.

Michael Seresin BSC

Cinematographer

Most cinematographers tend to film whatever is going on, and it doesn't really affect us. But *Midnight Express* with Alan Parker was quite tough. We had some really moving scenes—powerful scenes with actors giving everything—and it would be just me, the director, the operator and the ARRIFLEX 35BL 4 camera. It was like it became part of the family.

And it just worked; we never had any hiccups with it. Cameras were very simple then: it was the size, they were more compact, they were quieter for sound guys, they were easier to move around, and they were more flexible. The mechanics of filmmaking at that point were very, very efficient. So you had more time for directors to work with artists, for cinematographers to light and work out shots, and you got through more stuff.

My first experience with the ALEXA was when I shot the end and some extra bits on *Gravity*. When I saw the first print, it could easily have been film, and I do like things that look like film.

I was a bit dubious about digital as a principle because I like the tactile element of film; it's something tangible—you can see it and kiss it and hug it and smell it. But I shot a short film last year and they were dressing the set on location with candles, and the ALEXA camera was set up. I'm looking at the monitor and I hadn't put out one film light. I asked the props guy to put in another couple of candles here and there, and I said to the AD, "I'm ready." He said, "But you haven't lit it," and I said, "Yes I have." I shot a third of the film with no lights at all, literally just candles, and the quality was amazing. There's no film stock that could have done that, none that I'm aware of.

I shot a third of the film with no lights at all, literally just candles, and the quality was amazing.

Priya Seth IWCC

Cinematographer

I've been diving with scuba gear for about eight years and I shoot a lot of the Bollywood underwater sequences, in Bombay. Things like car crashes—people getting stuck in a car underwater and having to get out. I shoot these jobs with the ALEXA; before that it was film. We have this big underwater housing and we shoot in a pool that we make look like a studio, depending on the scene and the requirements. It's a very new industry in India, so we don't have the budgets and the kind of equipment that is available in the West.

Underwater, songs, narrative, action—as directors of photography we shoot everything.

I love to do it because every shoot is a completely new challenge. Not only do you have the variables of the camera and the lenses and the actors, but you've got water. The visibility in the water behaves like haze or fog, and there is the movement of the current if you are shooting in the sea. So every day is learning from zero and it's very exciting.

Underwater, songs, narrative, action—as directors of photography we shoot everything. Sometimes I feel that you get slotted for doing a particular thing, for example you're good at shooting skin commercials or good at shooting underwater, or hair. But I think we can all shoot anything, because at the end of the day we are making an image. So I like a big buffet.

Santosh Sivan ASC, ISC

Cinematographer

From an early age, my grandmother would encourage me to sketch. She used to teach in the palace; for me that was an early exercise in observing people and faces very closely. You find that not everyone is perfect, but it is the imperfection that makes something perfect.

My grandmother used to say, "This painting is an original," and my father, who taught me photography, would say, "The film negative is the original." Today we are in a digital world where everything is an original, like lighting a flame with another flame. Things are always changing, but I think your sensibilities do not change so much. Your inspiration is always rooted to your culture, and these roots provide our creative tree, with all its balance and vitality.

I love filming songs, because they are part of our culture. Long before cinema came into existence, puppet shows and dramas were accompanied by songs and music, in order to enhance the mood and the narration. It creates not just a movie experience, but also a festive aura. In their inception, movie songs were generally devotional, but over the years we rediscovered the art and now we have these songs in all kinds of situations—they have become a vital part of our cinemagoing experience. They are also a big publicity thing; like teaser trailers in Hollywood, in India there is an advance

Your inspiration is always rooted to your culture and these roots provide our creative tree.

audio release and sometimes the songs go viral. So in India we have our own signatures which distinguish us from the rest of the world and in some way make us immune to Hollywood.

Everyone has lived a different life and filled it with different experiences, and this makes art different for each of them. In a creative field, one plus one is not always two. It's about how much more one's sensibility can add.

Buddy Squires ASC

Cinematographer, Director

I love that documentary filmmaking gives me access to an incredible range of human experience. It allows me to intersect people at their most poignant moments.

I was off the coast of Libya working on a film called *The Last Hope*. We were filming the rescue of migrants who had escaped the jails of Libya only to be put to sea on cheap rubber rafts supplied by unscrupulous traffickers. To be out at dawn light in the middle of the Mediterranean and find a raft so packed with people that they have no room to move their arms—children, women and men desperately hoping that someone will save them before they run out of fuel, die from dehydration or drown as their flimsy raft sinks. To be present for that reality and to be able to bring it to an audience an ocean away is a huge responsibility and privilege.

The Last Hope was shot on the AMIRA, and the impact of bringing feature-film-quality imagery to these circumstances cannot be underestimated. The landscape of a three-year-old migrant child's face deserves to be photographed with the same care and attention I give to world leaders like the Dalai Lama or the iconic landscapes of nature. It is crucial that I imbue my portrayal of all people with as much dignity as I possibly can, and in the process elevate their stories to make their voices heard.

Super 16 mm film provided an amazing medium for documentaries. We could create gorgeous scenes with

very little technology and a small, lightweight package, anywhere in the world. There's something wonderful and magical about film that nothing replicates. But to shoot a project like *The Last Hope* with 16 mm would have been much more difficult. I didn't even have an assistant with me aboard the rescue ship, so I couldn't have efficiently used a film camera in that environment.

My work is about conveying truths that become obvious to my eye on location, making these revelations palpable and tactile for an audience—that is what cinematography allows me to do. Moving images of the world we inhabit have an incredible ability to reach across cultural boundaries, connecting our common humanity. Still, there are times I wish I was a writer and only had to have a pen and a pad with me, instead of carrying all this gear around.

It is crucial that I imbue my portrayal of all people with as much dignity as I possibly can.

Oliver Stapleton BSC

Cinematographer

My relationship with Stephen Frears began on several *Comic Strip* films that were each half an hour, shot on 16 mm. When *My Beautiful Laundrette* came up I thought Chris Menges would get the job because he had been working with Stephen up to that point, but Chris had just won an Oscar for *The Killing Fields* and he was asked to do *The Mission*, so I was the lucky man who got the job. That was the beginning of 15 years of shooting with Stephen.

When I was on the *Comic Strip* films, I was in a four-or five-year period of rock videos. So putting on a 6 mm ultra-wide lens was common for me, selecting low angles and handheld, and pushing the camera around the drummer, that was like my daily breakfast. When I started working with Stephen there was a particular moment where I was lying on the ground, lining up some crazy angle, and Stephen's face came into my view and he said, "What are you doing down there, dear boy?" And I remember saying, "This is a great angle," and he looked at me, and he didn't really blanch, he just said, "But will it tell the story?"

It was the realization that cinematography doesn't always–in fact rarely–need to be extravagant.

That was a key moment for me, because some very large penny dropped and I thought, "Oh, I see, I'm making a transition from rock 'n' roll pictures, which only last for two or three minutes, to storytelling, and the techniques required are completely different." I got up, dusted off my shirt, and said, "Well, so here?" And he went, "Yes, that'll do."

It was the realization that cinematography doesn't always –in fact rarely–need to be extravagant. Most of the time it should be invisible and tell the story. The problem with extravagant cinematography is that it draws attention to itself, whereas really great work draws you into its meaning. That was a road I started going down from that moment on.

Brendan Steacy CSC

Cinematographer

I love film and I was really reluctant to give up on it, but when the ALEXA came out there was a bit of a feeling of, "Well, it's very difficult to make my case against digital now," which was a bittersweet moment. I am still torn, emotionally. Film was kind of perfect in its imperfections.

I really love shooting digital in the dark. There's nothing there, but you're getting fantastic soft-dark things happening in the shadows. That bottom end, which was just at the edge of being usable on film, is the best part of the ALEXA's digital sensor.

Last year I did a film called *Lavender*. The story is a bit dark and we tried to represent that aesthetically, which is really fun for a cinematographer. I love the latitude of the ALEXA and the amount of room you have to play in, and underexposing things so massively—actually taking it so far that you start to get noise. When it starts to fall apart, then you can get something really lovely and that's where I think digital gets a bit magical.

I'm excited about how new technology will provide new opportunities for telling stories. When you imagine a scene, you imagine the coverage and the way you'd love something to be executed. We're often then forced to restrict that vision within the confines of what's available. So every time something new is introduced, you're removing restrictions on what your vision is.

I'm excited about how new technology will provide new opportunities for telling stories.

Rolf Steinmann

Cinematographer

After 10 years dreaming of this project, I was finally able to realize my short film *In Between* in 2015. Funded completely by myself, it offered me the chance to commit to my own ideas of a wildlife film, without compromise.

Musk oxen only live in the Arctic and have evolved for these cold, polar conditions. For me, they are a symbol of the fading ice age; they still exist, but the question is for how much longer. They are remnants from a different time, and I wanted the audience to experience that different age. On the one hand my film is about musk oxen, but for me it's more about the ice age that will probably be disappearing, soon.

I was in the middle of a storm and I didn't really know what to do.

The Arctic winter oscillates between two extremes: perfect silence and the rumbling noise of a storm. Only certain types of snowstorms are filmable; some are too violent and offer no visibility. Most of the time the musk oxen just wait for the storm to end, but for me that is exactly what made working with this species so fascinating. Nowadays cameras are always on the move, whereas I was going for the opposite: I wanted to film a static subject in a static way. I wanted motion, but inside the frame—not by moving the camera, but from the very elements of the Arctic winter.

There is a shot in my film where the musk oxen are standing there, very stoic, in a line. The storm is coming and they are disappearing in the snow and mist. This happened on the last day of my shoot, and it was a very sad moment for me; in some way it seemed symbolic. Perhaps I interpreted it too much, but they were fading away on my last day, and when I left them it touched me deeply.

The ALEXA never stopped working. The only problem was that the viewfinder fogged up. I was in the middle of a storm and I didn't really know what to do. I called the ARRI service team from the field and they told me to heat up the viewfinder with my camping stove. So I was heating it up over a fire, in the middle of nowhere. It got so hot that I couldn't touch it anymore without gloves, but it actually worked; the viewfinder was clean after that.

Tom Stern ASC, AFC

Cinematographer

I started working with Clint Eastwood in 1980, as a gaffer. I think it was in 2002—I had been lighting for about 35 years and was about to stop and do something else after the death of Conrad Hall—when Clint called and asked if I would shoot his next film. I said, "Well, thank you very much for calling. I only see two problems: one is I'm not in the camera union and secondly I know nothing about it." His response was, "Don't worry about the union, and you may know nothing about it, but at least it seems like you've been paying attention since 1980." I did a critical career analysis and thought, "Statistically I'm bound to fail and I'll need to leave the industry in shame and humiliation. But I'm leaving anyway, so there's really no downside." I decided I'd give it a spin; since then I think I've shot 30 pictures.

Clint is obsessed with blacks and I also like the blacks a lot, so for us it was always a matter of dynamic range.

Our first film with the ALEXA was *Jersey Boys*. We were having more and more trouble with the film infrastructure—the manufacturers, the laboratories, it was becoming more shaky, and Clint came to me and said, "What are the options here?" I had been testing the ALEXA; we'd shoot scenes with film and digital and do the color grade, and then we'd output to 35 mm print, and when it got to a point where you couldn't tell what you were looking at I said, "Well, there you go, it's seamless." Clint is obsessed with blacks and I also like the blacks a lot, so for us it was always a matter of dynamic range. The ALEXA, in my opinion, was basically the first camera to hit it.

Vittorio Storaro ASC, AIC

Cinematographer

When you consider your professional experience, knowledge, love, need—this is part of your life in the sense that every day, on any given assignment, you try to understand, through that experience, who you are.

If you want to go beyond the limits, you have to have confidence in the technology.

I am a cinematographer because I express myself through light and shadow. Bernardo Bertolucci helped me to reveal and understand myself. He has been into psychoanalysis since forever almost, and in his movies he often expresses himself by suggesting something through symbols. Bernardo would tell a story in a very conscious way, but sometimes he was using his unconscious to suggest an idea. At the same time I was using light in relation to the conscious side, and shadows for the unconscious. That was our journey together for 25 years.

If you want to go beyond the limits, you have to have confidence in the technology. First you have to love what you have in front of you. Even a mechanical element you have to love; even matter has a soul in my opinion, because to my mind without matter you can never have the energy to express yourself. Without a lens, without a camera, without film or a sensor, you cannot realize your idea.

Second, you have to trust the elements that you are using, otherwise you will never explore something new. It requires

humility and courage to go beyond, to become a visionary. You should never forget what Albert Einstein said: fantasy and imagination are sometimes much more important than knowledge. Of course, what we need to find is a balance between knowledge and imagination.

I'm now grateful to participate in two different eras.

Johnnie To

Director, Producer

I'm very fond of analog shooting. Nevertheless, I started to get acquainted with the new digital technology two or three years ago. I think in film history we can find situations that are comparable to today: silent movie actors and fans didn't appreciate the changes that the sound era brought, and there was a similar attitude when Technicolor was invented.

As a movie director I span the analog and digital ages, and even though I resisted the transformation at first, I'm now grateful to participate in two different eras. Future generations will not know the experience of analog filming. They will not know that making a mistake was sometimes like committing the most heinous crime, because there was no way of fixing it. They will not know the pleasant surprise of watching rushes that look completely different but much more exciting than expected.

Filmmaking has always been closely connected to technical developments. In the digital future, there will no longer be a boundary between imagination and realization.

Monika Treut

Director

I started making movies in the early 1980s, and there were very few women directors, producers or writers out there. I had to work with local companies in Hamburg and in the beginning I was treated quite badly. I vividly recall taking a film I had made to one of these companies, and they thought I was a production assistant, because they were not used to women filmmakers. They took the film print and said, "Okay, we got it. Goodbye." And I said, "Wait a minute, I'd like to stay and watch the color grading; I am the writer-producer-director." They really had trouble understanding this.

He was very proud that his first job in Germany was with ARRI, and he was just a total darling.

Then one day I had a very different experience, when ARRI opened an office in Hamburg. I was amazed because a young man came up to me, who actually was a refugee from Iran and who had just come to Germany. His German was already quite good and ARRI had given him this job, communicating with future clients, which I thought was wonderful. He was very proud that his first job in Germany was with ARRI, and he was just a total darling. He had no problems accepting me as a woman filmmaker; for him it was quite all right and fine, and even beautiful.

Tom Tykwer

Director

The first film I went to ARRI with was *Winter Sleepers*. It was a huge project for me at the time, just the format —Super 35—and with everything still analog.

One stylistic device I'd considered using for editing was long fades. I wanted everything to flow. But in those days you still used to sit at the editing table—the Steenbeck—and you could only do hard cuts. If you wanted a fade from one scene into another, the editor marked it directly on the film roll with a china marker, and you had this wavy wax line to imagine that one image merged into the next. *Winter Sleepers* had a huge number of fades, and countless long dissolves as well, and they were all just guesswork based on gut feel.

For someone to say, "We can do it better!"— I'd never experienced that before.

So, we spent almost a year editing. We kept chopping up the working copy and staring at the little screen until we finally thought: "Right! That'll just have to do!" Then we cut the negative, did some quick color grading and created the fades in the film lab, and now, for the first time, we were able to watch the so-called answer copy. And suddenly, there was the film on a large screen, in Cinemascope, with all the new colors. It was really exciting. There were people at ARRI who were really interested in the film, and for someone to say, "We can do it better!"— I'd never experienced

that before. I'd always been the only one saying, "Don't you think it could be better?" But now, people were coming to me. I would say, "Yeah, not bad," and they said: "No, no! That's not good enough. We can do it better." And it's still like that to this day.

It was strange when ARRI closed its film lab. It was like when a good friend passes away: even if they're very old, it's still sad. You miss them, but you know that life's like that. For me, going digital–from the filming, through editing, to the final picture–makes things so much easier, with so many improvements, that I don't even think about film anymore.

Koichi Uematsu

Executive Engineer, Technical Operations, Technical Department, Fuji Television Network, Inc.

My goal is to create an atmosphere for artists. I'm lighting for music and entertainment shows, and usually I give the singers a natural look.

When I had the idea to make a "full LED studio," I did a lot of research. I tested different brands from manufacturers all over the world. I wanted to have the best lights, and the ARRI SkyPanels offered the most options to me. I can easily match them with different lighting sources such as tungsten, so I can react to any situation.

I always try to explain to my students that it's not just about lighting technology. There is no formula; it's always about the idea. They should focus on what they want to do and then they should think about how they can implement their concept. I don't teach methods; I provide a place where people can think. I set up different situations and let them feel those situations. I try to motivate them and I hope that they will find their own way. That's the point.

I wanted to have the best lights.

Jost Vacano BVK, ASC

Cinematographer

With feature films, I always preferred a documentary approach. I wanted the viewers to be drawn into it in a more direct way; that's why I have a weakness for handheld camerawork.

Back then, in the early 1970s, there was no such thing as the Steadicam. I had to try to figure something out for myself, and I came up with the principle of the gyro-compass. The American Marines had something like it in their binoculars, to stabilize them as the ship rolls on the waves. So I got hold of one of these parts and I screwed it to the bottom of my ARRIFLEX 35 IIB, which I had bought secondhand in the late 1950s. Of course the stabilizer doesn't balance out all the movement–that's not possible. You can still see that the cameraman is walking, but it's not distracting, and that's exactly what I wanted.

This camera was simply an extension of my body.

Then there was the issue of the viewfinder. At that time it stuck straight out at the back, but I really wanted a camera where I could also look down into the eyepiece at an angle. So I said to ARRI, "Just take your X-ray camera" –it was the same basic model–"and add the magnifier from the viewfinder of the ARRIFLEX 35 III; cut it off somehow, and glue it in place." They said it wasn't going to be that easy, but they worked with the idea and that's how the ARRIFLEX 35 IIIC came into being, with the swivel-mounted viewfinder. During the filming of

Das Boot (*The Boat*), it was still a prototype, and afterwards ARRI said, “Come on, we’re going to take the prototype back, and we’ll give you a new one.” And I took that one to America with me.

This camera was simply an extension of my body. I continued to use it in America, along with many other ARRI cameras, and it came to be known as the Josticam.

Kees van Oostrum ASC

Cinematographer

In 2006 the museum at Mount Vernon, which was the house of George Washington, decided to make a half-hour movie that they could show. I got the assignment to direct a real Hollywood version of George Washington, which meant a big canvas and beautiful shots. This was an example of the ASC being a wonderful resource, because there are all these experienced people there. I went to Richard Edlund, who is an Oscar-winning visual effects cameraman, and I said, "I want to do something that is visually absolutely stunning, because this film is going to show for a long time and I want people to really experience the man in the landscape." Richard told me I should shoot it on 65 mm, and I remember saying, "What is that?" He explained that it was an older format, but that it was really terrific and I should try it out.

We did some tests, and I was really blown away by the large format.

I looked around and the ARRIFLEX 765 was available, so we did some tests, and I was really blown away by the large format. In the end, *We Fight To Be Free* was a mixture of 65 mm and 35 mm because I had to shoot all the winter landscapes and the bigger shots in the winter, before I was able to cast the actors. I went out with the 765 in the winter and we shot these big plate shots, although they weren't just plate shots, they had movement and people in them. Then in the summer I shot the actors in 35 mm and sort of composited them in; it became a photographic compilation. When it came out I showed it to some people and they thought it had an immense, beautiful quality, which was what I wanted. Today 65 mm has become a very sought-after format.

SCENE
ROLL
100 YEARS OF
PROD
A. TRAN
DIR
S. CVETKO
CAM

DF
TAKE
1
FPS
24.00
CAM
A/B
DATE
02/06/17

Checco Varese ASC

Cinematographer

I never thought I would be a cinematographer. I studied architecture in Italy and came back to Peru, but there was no work due to economic crisis number 428 of the decade —nobody was building anything. A friend of mine had an adventure travel company, and they got a phone call saying they needed a guy that spoke English and knew the Amazon region, because National Geographic was doing a documentary about the origins of the Amazon River.

It was the first time I ever saw a film camera. I remember it precisely: the date was March 27, 1982, and it was an ARRIFLEX 16SR 2. The camera assistant got sick and the cameraman said, "This is a magazine, you put it here and it goes 'clunk.' If it doesn't go 'clunk' it's not fed in, then you push here and it grabs the film and goes like that." Okay, great. "Then you have to change the film." I was like, "I have to change the film? I'm just the guy that translates." He says, "No, you have to change the film." So the producer, the cameraman and myself ended up on the Amazon for three months.

I think there is an analogy between a cinematographer and an architect.

I think there is an analogy between a cinematographer and an architect. Architects do not build walls; architects build spaces. Cinematographers do not light walls; they light spaces. You need to understand color. You need to understand space. A floor plan needs to flow just like the blocking of a scene needs to flow. Architects frame constantly—you do a drawing in order to show how it's going to look, and it is a frame. The analogy is there, so it was a wonderful transition for me.

Joseph Vilsmaier BVK

Cinematographer, Director

When I was a kid, I wanted to be a fireman, a racing cyclist or a cameraman. So in 1953 I started an apprenticeship in camera precision mechanics at ARRI. It was an absolutely wonderful time, although it was also very hard because we had to work long hours, even on Saturdays. But we were a close-knit team: apprentices, fellows, master craftsmen all together—it was really terrific.

August Arnold was incredibly industrious. He would drive to Hamburg by car early in the morning and back again at 3 a.m. I remember the gatekeeper always had a snack with him, and Mr. Arnold would say, at three in the morning, "Did you leave some for me?" Usually, there was Leberkäse (a kind of meatloaf). I'm sure the gatekeeper always brought a second helping because he knew Mr. Arnold would be hungry when he got back.

In 1953 I started an apprenticeship in camera precision mechanics at ARRI.

In 1961 I finished my training at ARRI, passed the precision mechanic's exam with an A, and went to Bavaria, where I worked as an assistant to Gernot Roll for 10 years. We were a great team.

I have a favorite project that I've been dreaming of for a decade. I don't know whether it's going to come to anything, but I've already approached Gernot about it.

"We could make a final film together—we're the same age," I said. "We could share the work 50/50, and you're the better cameraman anyway." I don't think we'd end up clashing with one another, because in all the time we've known each other, we haven't had one argument. We always said, straight away: "Forget it! We'll discuss it tomorrow," and the next day, we'd laugh about it and agree that we'd got ourselves into a knot over nothing.

Amy Vincent ASC

Cinematographer

One of the things that will always be part of a person —an artist and an artist's legacy—is the people who trained them and the people that they in turn reach out a hand to, and train, and bring along.

I came up working under a lot of amazing cameramen, like Robert Richardson, Bill Pope, John Lindley and Dariusz Wolski. So I had quite an education. And while I was working as a camera assistant I went back to school, to the American Film Institute. It was then that I realized how much I had learned just by being on set alongside some of cinema's masters.

Cinematography is still an incredibly male-dominated profession. I am one of a small number of women who actually have the privilege, training and experience to do this job, but the numbers are changing and the energy and the power is shifting. Initially I was inspired to become a teacher alongside my cinematography career for that very reason. We must start with education if we're going to increase the numbers of female cinematographers working in today's workforce, although it's very important to me that we drop "female cinematographer" as part of our language. We are all cinematographers.

To me, right now in my life, what drives me most is the legacy of young people that I get to spend time with; I help them find their artistic voice through education. There is nothing more rewarding.

We must start with education if we're going to increase the numbers of female cinematographers.

Jan Weincke DFF

Cinematographer

I remember working on a black-and-white film when I was employed as a camera assistant at a studio, and I decided that at least once in my life I'd like to shoot a black-and-white feature film. I went on to do a lot of films for Nils Malmros and every time I said, "Listen, we should do it in black-and-white," and he said, "No, I don't like it so much."

I kept asking, and finally he was going to do a film about the life of his father, who was born just before the First World War, and I said, "This is black-and-white," and he agreed.

The producers of *Facing the Truth* were not happy with this decision; they asked us to shoot in color and just make black-and-white prints. I refused to do that because black-and-white needs a different way of lighting. If you have a person in a dark sweater in front of a black background, you have to have some backlights. When I shoot in color, I never use backlight because it is not natural light, but on black-and-white it gives you the shape and splits the person from the background. I generally like soft light, but in this film I sometimes used direct light because the black-and-white needed a little power.

In the story there was a party, with all these women dressed up in the finest clothes. The girl who made the dresses had really worked hard making these beautiful, colorful things, but I started getting scared because in the darkness they were very alike. We shot a test and five of the dresses looked completely the same color, so we had to change them. We made charts with colors and the corresponding black-and-white tones next to each other, so everybody could see that if you chose this red, you got this level of darkness in the film. These charts were used by the production designers and costumiers, and that solved the problem.

Black-and-white needs a different way of lighting.

Wim Wenders

Director

When I was a film student in Munich in the late 1960s, I owned a used Bolex 16 mm camera. Like any other film student, I dreamed of making a gangster film as my first effort. But my means were extremely limited; I could just afford one reel of black-and-white negative film. I absolutely wanted to make a tracking shot, so my friend Hanns Zischler ran down the street holding a machine gun, or rather, stumbled down the street as if he was dying. (This must have been heavily influenced by Godard's *À bout de souffle.*) I was driving alongside in my Citroën 2CV. That car had the advantage that you could open the roof and shoot out of it, which gave you a relatively high angle, so I decided to only film my actor from his waist down. You never see his face. I was so fascinated by the way he dragged himself along that I used the entire reel on it. Well, it was only four minutes long. I took my negative to ARRI, which was the first time I'd ever set foot in a film lab. They developed the negative for me and printed it once. That pretty much ate up my entire budget. I realized that one couldn't possibly make a film from that little snippet.

I was a passionate pinball player at the time. Not far from ARRI, down along Tuerkenstrasse, there was a legendary pub called the "Bungalow" where all the Munich film types hung out. They had two pinball machines and I was a real pinball wizard. If you played a good game, a sign would light up: "Same Player Shoots Again" and you would get an extra ball. That became the inspiration for what I was going to do with my single shot.

I took my bit of black-and-white negative to ARRI again and asked them to print it four more times, but please, this time, color the prints in monochromatic blue, red, yellow and green. Those were my special effects, my extra balls. They just stared at me in disbelief, as they had never received a job like that before. "Okay, so you mean four rushes, one in each color?" It took a couple of days and once again cost an awful lot of money. Then one night I sat down at the only editing room in film school and joined the four colored film strips together. The film consists of just that one sequence, colored differently each time, like three balls in a pinball game with the extra fourth … plus a title card I shot on a friend's 10-second leftover film.

The original print of the film ran at festivals and God knows where. I didn't have the money for any more prints, so I showed my original. Of course, it got scratched more and more in the course of time. I didn't have the money to make a new negative from that one badly damaged print. As it was, I had already spent everything I had at ARRI, just to get that first piece of negative developed and printed, and then to have it colored four times. So the film was shown over and over again until it was in shreds. Luckily, the one and only print eventually ended up at the Munich Film Museum. They felt pity for the raggedy piece of film and saved it by having a new negative made from it—again at ARRI, of course.

I had already spent everything I had at ARRI, just to get that first piece of negative developed and printed, and then to have it colored four times.

Arthur Wong HKSC

Cinematographer, Director, Producer

Much to my regret, I'm not entirely pleased with any of my work. You notice your flaws only when you're watching your film together with an audience. I often say to myself, "I won't do it this way next time."

Sleepless Town is reasonably satisfactory, but there's this one flaw I can never forget. The opening sequence is a single take that lasts for five minutes, and our camera operator was drained of all energy after using up the first roll of film. The camera went all the way into Kabukicho, a red-light district in Shinjuku, Tokyo, which could have happened only once in film history. We asked the triads to help us make sure things wouldn't go wrong. Not the police—that's beyond them. At the critical moment, they cordoned off a crossroads for our shoot. A huge crane hauled down a makeshift elevator from above. The camera operator ran a long way before getting into the elevator, capturing the *Sleepless Town* signboard hung somewhere between the second and third floor. At that moment, the film turned from black-and-white to color.

I struggled for a long time whether I should use that take, but it was our only option.

The shot continued until the rooftop apartment of the main character, played by Takeshi Kaneshiro, came into frame. We couldn't use Steadicam but only a handheld camera, and that's the only take we got. But while following

Kaneshiro on the run, the camera got a bit too close and its shadow can be seen on his back. The industry veterans grumbled, "What? Textbook shot? Can't you see the huge shadow of the camera?" But there was no CGI back then, no means to wipe it off. I struggled for a long time whether I should use that take, but it was our only option. After the shot, the exhausted camera operator slumped to the ground, gasping. I even gave him a massage! I had no choice but to use the take—though not without regrets.

Du Yan

Producer

I Am a Singer is a Chinese reality TV show on which talented, well-known singers compete with each other, singing new songs adapted from old ones. Five hundred live audience members cast their vote for their favorite singer.

We have high standards for image quality. For season three we wanted a more cinematic look, so we did a lot of testing on different cameras. Our director of photography shot some material with the ARRI AMIRA and showed me the images. I immediately realized that this was exactly what we were looking for. Using this kind of camera was unprecedented in Chinese TV, so I asked the head of Hunan Television if we could use the cinema cameras, and he fully supported us. He told us we were more than welcome to try and innovate. In the end, season three of *I Am a Singer* looked totally unique in terms of its image quality, compared with traditional TV shows.

We decided we wanted a more cinematic look.

On most of the episodes we used AMIRA to shoot the reality-show sections, but for the finale we used 23 AMIRAs for a live broadcast, which grabbed a lot of industry attention. For the next season we took the characteristics of AMIRA into the design process. Its color reproduction is one of the very best out there. We are always looking to try new things.

Katsumi Yanagijima JSC

Cinematographer

I put a lot of effort into the whole concept of a film and then I just shoot. I think it is important not to stick too much to the script.

Zatoichi is a blind Japanese swordsman. The character is very well known because he featured in all these classic series of samurai films and television dramas. It was a discussion as to whether we should film a remake or not, and if we did it, director Takeshi Kitano was anxious to create something nobody had ever seen before.

Kitano had the idea of putting a tap-dance sequence in a samurai movie long before we started filming *Zatoichi*. We had an exceptionally large amount of rehearsals for this tap-dance scene, done with Japanese wooden sandals. In the end it only took five or six hours to shoot, using three cameras.

In general, I use only two or three lenses, mostly a 28 mm, 35 mm and 50 mm. I rarely use a focal length greater than 85 mm, and I do not use zoom lenses. On each film I try to shoot differently; if there are many action scenes, I might combine a wide-angle lens with a long lens to emphasize the speed of the action, but I always seem to come back to my method of restricting myself to three lenses. I think that when you set limits, inspiration comes more easily.

I always seem to come back to my method of restricting myself to three lenses.

Steve Yedlin ASC

Cinematographer

I went to film school, but I really developed a passion for cinema by making homemade movies with my buddy Rian Johnson, who I met during my last year at high school. Even back then there was such a lot of thought behind his visual storytelling, where all the components are working together for the narrative. Since then, I've done all of his feature films.

Star Wars: The Last Jedi had the most useful prep of any movie I've ever done, in terms of using the time in an effective way: everything from really talking to the production and set designers about lighting to mapping

out SkyPanels. I spent weeks with a SkyPanel, a media server and an ALEXA in my office, mapping out the chromaticity coordinates for all the colors we might want.

Another example of good use of the time was the rigorous building of our show LUTs, which included shooting dense data sets on both film and ALEXA. There's a strange presumption that shooting film just works and you don't have to build a LUT for it, but I actually spent more time getting film to look like film than getting ALEXA to look like film. Scanned film has on the one hand been rephotographed by a second camera (the scanner) and on the other hand has not been contact-printed. So if the goal is the color and contrast of printed film, then scanned film's starting point is as far from the goal as digital camera files.

I do not believe that the tools enforce an aesthetic look.

I do not believe that the tools enforce an aesthetic look. There is a very deep belief that the technical and aesthetic are utterly tied together, and I think this has been made a self-fulfilling prophecy by people not paying enough attention to the process that happens between the camera and the final image. To me the most important thing about a camera system is technical, because I am going to define my own aesthetics no matter which camera I use. And ARRI has been the most technically sound system in terms of hardware and software, but also openness and not putting obfuscation into the marketplace.

Marek Żydowicz

Festival Director, Camerimage

The Camerimage Film Festival was born 25 years ago. It is an event dedicated to the art of cinematography. During the festival we present the work of artists from all over the world, both masters and students. I am an art historian, and I taught at the University of Toruń for 15 years. In 1991, I prepared an exhibition devoted to neo-expressionism. I had the idea of a European cross-genre approach and invited Volker Schlöndorff with his film *Voyager*. He was very shy, seeing all these paintings by famous artists such as Anselm Kiefer, Georg Baselitz and Jörg Immendorff. During the presentation of his film, Volker was sitting outside the room, and afterwards he said to me, "I invite you to the pub this evening, we must talk." In the course of this conversation he told me this: "Marek, you must find a special idea for a film event." "What kind of event?" "This is your problem. If you have an idea, please call me."

> I sent two faxes, one to Sven Nykvist and the other to Vittorio Storaro.

Two years later I called him and asked, "What about a festival devoted to the art of cinematography?" He was excited: "This is a fantastic concept, Marek; it's great. You must ask some famous cinematographers what they think." I sent two faxes, one to Sven Nykvist and the other to Vittorio Storaro. Sven was the first to accept the invitation. One hour later, I got a fax from Vittorio, and the first sentence was, "I hate you Mr. Żydowicz because you had this idea, not me, but I agree; I'll be at Camerimage when it takes place for the first time."

Colophon

Published by:
Hirmer Verlag GmbH
Nymphenburger Str. 84
80636 Munich

Edited by:
ARRI AG
Türkenstr. 89
80799 Munich

Concept and compilation:
Henning Rädlein

Text:
Mark Hope-Jones
Sophie Kill

Art direction:
Sylvia Rädlein

Cover photo:
Jan Heugel

Interviewers:
Volker Bahnemann, Aleksej Berkovic, Augustine Cheung, Natasza Chroscicki, Judith Evans, Jon Fauer ASC, Robert Fischer, Nicolai Fitzgerald, Hao He, Mark Hope-Jones, Sun-Cho Jeon, Mamoru Kagami, Tiger Kang, Franz Kraus, Jens Meurer, Tony Ngai, Meinhard Pril, Henning Rädlein, Magrét Rún, Yoshio Shimizu, Brett Smith, An Tran

Images:
Shahram Aderangui, Julien Adreetti, Pierre Assenat, Byung-Seok BAE, Andreas Berkl, Aleksej Berkovic RGC, Anian Bernrieder, Richard Blanchard, Philipp Chudalla, Svetlana Cvetko, Florian Dittel, Sean Dooley, Tom Fährmann BVK, Thomas Gottschalk, Birgit Guðjónsdóttir BVK IKS, Chase Hagen, Dicky Ho, Alexandre Ilkhovski RGC, Lotta Kilian, Tae-Jung KIM, Jana Lämmerer, Johannes Louis, Pierre Martinet, Theresa Maué, Ahmed El Nagar, Lukas Nicolaus, Henning Rädlein, Josh Salzman, Logan Schneider, Thomas Schneider, An Tran, Rick Tullis, Tilmann Wittneben, Paul Yee

Transcription:
MSS Kapstadt – Die Sprachenagentur

Proofreading:
Rita Forbes, Munich

ARRI project management:
Rosi Rothenfußer

Hirmer project management:
Rainer Arnold

Layout:
Peter Grassinger

Pre-press and repro:
Reproline Genceller, Munich

Printing:
Passavia Druckservice, Passau

Paper:
GardaMatt Ultra

Printed in Germany

Bibliographic information published by the Deutsche Nationalbibliothek: The Deutsche Nationalbibliothek lists this publication in the Deutsche Nationalbibliografie; detailed bibliographic data is available on the Internet at http://www.dnb.de.

ISBN 978-3-7774-2857-4

www.arri.com
www.hirmerpublishers.com

ARRI

The Filmmaker's View

100 YEARS OF ARRI

HIRMER

Contents

Foreword

ARRI, Artisans and Artists

Interviews

Foreword

The Stahl family

This book draws on just some of the more than 200 video interviews ARRI conducted with international filmmakers in the lead-up to its centenary celebrations in 2017. The interviews contained herein are a representative sample, collectively giving an impression of the project's diversity and scope. Think of this as an initial release—volume one of a larger, ongoing publishing effort. We extend profound thanks to the many filmmakers who gave up their time to support this undertaking, and we encourage readers to visit the ARRI website, where all of the interviews can be viewed.

There have been countless key moments over the last 100 years, many of which might be seen as having been pivotal. In the early years, when August Arnold and our forebear Robert Richter were youngsters, they developed the first devices themselves. Above all they were camera operators, and the reason they were able to conceive technical improvements to the equipment was because they were using it every day.

When Erich Kästner joined in the early 1930s, the company moved into a second phase. Up to that point the products were more or less assembled at the workbench, without any real plan, but Mr. Kästner ushered in a true process of design. The first camera he built was the ARRIFLEX 35, with its reflex shutter, and he was the driving force behind many further cameras over subsequent decades. Among the last he worked on were the 35BL, which allowed ARRI to start fully meeting the needs of feature films, and the 16SR, which introduced symmetrical design.

From the moment Kästner began at ARRI, the company's success has really been down to its employees. There was a period of transition after he left, having worked into his 80s, but a third phase came with the rise of Franz Kraus, who started out in the fledgling video department. He became general manager and when we restructured in 2001—separating the owners from day-to-day operations—he was made a managing director and board member of the newly formed ARRI AG. Over the years his technical influence has been tremendous; it was he who pushed the board to approve the ARRILASER and ARRISCAN, which was the right decision because it taught us what the digital industry requires, setting us down a path that eventually led to the ALEXA.

Within these three broad phases of ARRI history there have of course been innumerable other employees who, through their ideas and efforts, played vital roles in the company's achievements. Today the core DNA of ARRI is simply that it is a place where people enjoy their work. There are so many smart and talented individuals on the team, and ARRI provides an environment where they can pursue their ideas, take on responsibility, make their own decisions and fulfil their potential. Amazingly, after 100 years, when you walk through ARRI you get a sense that the staff has the same spirit as the founders did, so it's very hands-on, with lots of freedom. People feel inspired, and that is the best way to keep attracting the right employees.

While we take little credit for ARRI's accomplishments over recent years, we do believe that being a family-owned company continues to benefit ARRI and the people who work there. Without the distractions of short-term financial accountability to public shareholders, we do not have to be overly concerned with the profitability of each and every development. We can afford to let the company develop the right portfolio of products and make investments that keep it going in the right direction, because over the long term this is how to maintain our brand identity, which in the end brings its own rewards.

Keeping our attention on long-term goals allows for an unwavering focus on the real needs of customers. Culturally, ARRI has always sought to supply and add value, rather than just extracting it, and this is a key part of our formula for success. The single most essential asset of the company is how it is perceived within the filmmaking community. Over its lifetime ARRI has built up a solid reputation for product reliability and fair treatment of its customers. Such trust is very difficult to acquire, and very easy to lose.

User feedback has always been the most crucial element in developing the right tools for filmmakers, so it is entirely fitting that the story of ARRI should be told in this book—and in the wider project of which it forms part—through the voices of the company's end users. It is they who have inspired the products and services, and they who have made them a success. So, enough of our words, we hope you enjoy theirs.

ARRI, Artisans and Artists

Jon Fauer ASC

ARRI was founded a century ago by two aspiring cinematographers who appreciated the value of technology in the pursuit of their dreams. The excellent adventure of August Arnold and Robert Richter reads like a good screenplay. There is a dramatic arc, with competition, conflict, struggle against odds, stumbles, success and celebration. Serendipity helped, along with good business sense. They were involved in all fields of film production —from manufacturing cameras, lights, and lenses to managing post and rentals.

The centennial celebration of the connections between cinematography and ARRI is a story about artists and artisans, technique and technology, creativity and tools. Collecting ephemeral images inside a dark box is an intertwined intersection of art and machine. Making these machines is also an art—and it is a remarkable achievement for one family-owned enterprise to have successfully engaged in that pursuit for a hundred years. ARRI is among a handful of equipment companies founded at the birth of cinema that continue to this day: Carl Zeiss (ZEISS) 1846, Ernst Leitz (Leica) 1849, Taylor Hobson (Cooke) 1886, Kodak 1888, Gaumont 1895, Pathé 1896, Éclair 1907 and Vinten 1910.

August Arnold was born on September 12, 1898, son of an Austrian arborist. Robert Richter was born a year later in Nuremberg; his family owned the sanitary and heating wholesale trading company of Richter+Frenzel (founded in 1895 and still running today). The boys met as classmates in 1913 at the Oskar-von-Miller High School in Munich. Their hobbies were movies and mechanical things. Christmas came with a motorized lathe that was soon put to good use modifying an old slide projector to watch discarded newsreels and short film clips. A couple of years later, still in school, the two aspiring cinematographers bought a Gaumont hand-cranked camera. When not in class, they worked as camera assistants and also as cameramen covering the news. The boys often scooped stories by racing around on their bicycles to get more angles than their competitors.

On September 12, 1917, August Arnold and Robert Richter founded ARRI in a small shop on Tuerkenstrasse in Munich to satisfy an eclectic assortment of interests, as announced on their business cards: "Fine mechanics, electrical devices, arc lamps, film apparatus, film printers, camera operating and projection." Their first products were movie lights and printing machines. In the beginning, the boys were not even old enough to legally sign their business documents. One hundred years later, the company they started is still located at the same address, now much larger, with 1,400 employees worldwide.

It's helpful to look through the prism of history, artistic trends and industrial influence. By the time Arnold and Richter set up their first shop on Tuerkenstrasse, cinema had been flourishing for 22 years. About 740 km southwest of Munich, Auguste and Louis Lumière built a small, lightweight, portable Cinématograph that combined the tasks of shooting, printing and projecting 35 mm film transported by an intermittent movement inspired by sewing machines that were widely manufactured in their native city of Lyon. Their short documentaries were celebrations of the mechanized society being depicted: workers leaving the factory, a train arriving in a station. 6,494 km to the west, Thomas Edison's camera was nicknamed the "Black Maria." It was the size of a house and rotated on tracks to film static scenes of sneezes, magicians, politicians, dancers and scantily-clad women.

From the beginning, differences between European and US productions influenced equipment design. Budgets in the US were bigger and large studio cameras, supported by rugged dollies and big cranes, could be managed by larger crews. The Hollywood studio system influenced a style of its own, while in Europe smaller budgets generally engendered a leaner production style, with smaller crews and more compact equipment.

Technique and technology in filmmaking has been a chicken and egg confabulation since the beginning. Does the idea come first and then you look for the equipment to get the shot? Or is it the other way around—an innovative new piece of gear inspires a new way to tell the story? It's a combination of both, streamlining the steps from script to screen. This was the world in which August Arnold and Robert Richter grew up as youngsters. Their instinctive proclivity to get involved in all facets of cinema, not just building cameras or being cameramen, most likely helped in their success. It was the inception of an industry that would introduce universal ideas to more people than ever before, the democratization and globalization of an art form that would be seen by the largest audiences in history. The founders of ARRI set off on a cinematic path of eclectic invention to support a hobby that became a successful business conceived in a nimble, mobile, European style of production.

Two years after the founding of ARRI and one year after the end of World War I, Austin Lescarboura wrote in *Behind the Motion Picture Screen* (1919, Scientific American Publishing Company), "Out of the miles of celluloid depicting battles has sprung a new brotherhood of nations lately. Who knows but that the motion picture will continue to aid in the greatest of all things on earth in the future—the reunion of all nations into a real league of nations? The fact is that the cameraman is an artist; but instead of pigments and brushes he relies on various mechanical contraptions. Now, if ever there was an ingenious individual it is the expert cameraman; for starting out with the camera as turned over to him by the motion-picture engineers, he has forever been busy improving its mechanism and developing any number of accessories."

In Munich, Arnold and Richter were busy improving mechanisms, building printing machines and lighting equipment, and renting out their own cameras in between jobs to colleagues—pretty much the same things ARRI still does today. They also shot and acted in early German Westerns, with lugubrious titles like *Vengeance in the Valley of Gold* and *Deadly Cowboys*, in the nearby Bavarian forests. In 1924, they built their first camera, the KINARRI 35. It had a pancake body shape like the Akeley, hand-cranked with 100' loads. Next came the KINARRI Model II Tropic, with an adjustable rotary shutter and a daylight film magazine. These were basically intended for the proliferating 35 mm amateur market. Richter was convinced that 16 mm would be more suitable for home movies, and the KINARRI 16 followed soon after.

Robert Richter visited America in 1925, selling ARRI equipment and working as a waiter at the Commodore Hotel in New York, at the Hollywood labs of Fox and Lasky, and then as a camera assistant at Universal. He could not have avoided noticing how the Hollywood studio system encouraged bigger and heavier cameras. Richter's observations undoubtedly influenced ARRI camera designs after he returned to Munich, enrolled at the Munich Technological University and received a degree in engineering.

Mitchell built their first BNC ("Blimped Newsreel Camera") in 1932. It was hardly a newsreel camera. At 120 lb, it was a gigantic silent camera intended for feature production. Technicolor's first 3-strip camera was also introduced in 1932, and was built by Mitchell as well.

ARRI's big breakthrough in camera design weighed a mere 13.5 lb (6.1 kg) and had a spinning mirror for reflex viewing. It was introduced as a prototype in 1936 and as a production-ready product at the 1937 Leipzig Fair. The ARRIFLEX 35 had a WYSIWYG image: what you saw on the ground glass was identical to the image captured on film, parallax free, and able to show whether the shot was in or out of focus. Erich Kästner, having joined ARRI at age 21 in 1933, was the chief design engineer of this lightweight, small and rugged camera. From this point on, writers were obliged to distinguish between ARRI the company and ARRIFLEX—the cameras with reflex viewing via spinning mirror shutters.

Austin Lescarboura's hope that motion pictures would encourage "the reunion of all nations" was shattered by the horror of yet another war, and many miles of celluloid once again depicted battles and cinematographers once again became combat cameramen during World War II. German combat cameramen used ARRIFLEX 35 cameras. The Americans had Bell & Howell Eyemos. The first ARRIFLEX 35s came to America as captured cameras via the US Army Pictorial Center in Queens, New York. Word of the spinning mirror and reflex viewing spread.

ARRI's factory in Munich was totally destroyed by Allied bombs in 1944, but manufacturing had been moved to the Bavarian countryside several years earlier. The next-generation ARRIFLEX 35 II went into production in 1941; after the war it gained attention in the US for handheld, MOS, documentary and POV shots. A 35 II was used extensively on *Louisiana Story* (1948), directed by Robert Flaherty and shot by Richard Leacock, a pioneer of Direct Cinema and Cinéma Vérité. Tonino Delli Colli AIC shot *The Good, the Bad and the Ugly* (1966), starring Clint Eastwood, with a 35 IICT/B Techniscope 2-perf (2.35:1 aspect ratio) camera. It used half as much film as 4-perf anamorphic, reducing costs and increasing time between reloads. More than 17,000 ARRIFLEX 35 cameras (including its variants: IIA, IIB, IIC) were sold through 1979, when it was replaced by the ARRIFLEX 35 III.

In 1951, ARRI appointed Paul Klingenstein and Kling Photo in New York to be their exclusive importer for the US. But it was still like the Wild West, with various independent agents, including a drugstore in Atlanta, selling ARRI cameras.

Television news and documentaries were increasingly shot in 16 mm. The ARRIFLEX 16ST was introduced in 1950, based on the same spinning mirror shutter concept as the 35 II. It took 100' spools that could be loaded in daylight, much like the Bell & Howell Filmo, and also accepted 400' magazines. The 16ST was followed by the 16M (magazine only, no daylight spools); then the 16BL arrived in 1965 for 16 mm sync sound documentary and industrial film production. It was ARRI's first silent camera.

By this time, more than 1,300 employees worked at ARRI around Munich—running the film labs and building camera, lighting, processing and printing equipment. The workforce was well educated and skilled. Munich was, and still is, an epicenter of fine mechanics and precision engineering—partly due to a rigorous apprenticeship program. The first task of an aspiring ARRI apprentice was to file, by hand, a piece of steel into a perfect cube. This took about six weeks. Next, the apprentices had to cut a triangular opening in one piece of metal, and a corresponding triangular solid from another piece. The closer they fit together, the better was deemed that person's potential for success at ARRI.

La nouvelle vague, the French New Wave, arguably began with Truffaut's *The 400 Blows* (1959), shot by Henri Decaë, and Jean-Luc Godard's *Breathless* (1960), shot by Raoul Coutard AFC. Both used Éclair Caméflex cameras. Raoul Coutard recalled, "Jean-Luc had promised to make the film cheaply. To make a good film on a small budget sacrifices had to be made: no sound-stages, no lighting, no heavy cameras—to cut down on grip equipment. We needed new technology to make the film."

It took almost a decade to drag Hollywood out of their studios and onto location. In 1968, William A. Fraker ASC shot *Bullitt*, directed by Peter Yates and starring Steve McQueen. "We used ARRIFLEXes all the way through, and we destroyed some, but they held up absolutely beautifully for the most part," Fraker said a few years before he passed away. "I was also one of the first people [in Hollywood] to use a blimped ARRIFLEX. We had to import it from New York, because Hollywood didn't have any. It was a smaller piece of equipment and we shot on actual locations in San Francisco, like seedy hotels on the waterfront—we just didn't have the room to put big equipment in."

Next came *Easy Rider* (1969), shot by László Kovács ASC with Vilmos Zsigmond's personal ARRIFLEX 35 IIC. The film's exuberant, documentary, handheld, flared-lens, new-wave style triggered the New Hollywood era of filmmaking in the early 1970s. This American New Wave was enabled by the technology of the cameras that created the spontaneous style—but economics decided where the industry was heading next. *Easy Rider* was the third highest grossing film of 1969. With a low budget around $360,000, it made $60 million worldwide. If you were a Hollywood mogul, you saw dollar signs in the future of low-budget, independent productions. If you were a camera manufacturer, you would be scrambling to outfit cinematographers with the tools to shoot those new movies.

ARRI launched the ARRIFLEX 35BL in 1972, the company's first silent 35 mm production camera. The need for such a camera had been strongly expressed by Paul Klingenstein and Volker Bahnemann in the US. Having started as an apprentice at Kling Photo in the late 1960s, Bahnemann had by this point risen to VP of Marketing. In 1978 he would become president of Arnold and Richter's first subsidiary outside of Germany, ARRI Inc. Today he sits on the Supervisory Board of ARRI AG.

Designed by Joachim Gerb and Erich Kästner, the 35BL rested comfortably on the operator's shoulder. At 33 lb, and around 33 dB, it required a lens blimp for silence, but was light, small and portable. Unveiled at the 1972 Munich Summer Olympic Games, it appeared to be intended as a 35 mm silent newsreel and sports camera with the ability to toggle between sync sound and a top speed of 100 fps for slow motion. Of course, it could do much more than that. In the US, Jack Priestley ASC was one of the first to use a 35BL, on *Across 110th Street* (1972). Priestley described the camera: "It was as quiet as a church mouse and had great flexibility. I don't know what I would have done in a lot of spots without it, especially in those small rooms where we often had to shoot. You put it on your shoulder and could walk around, bend down, sit down, hold it in your lap."

Iterations of the 35BL followed, project-managed by Otto Blaschek, who had joined ARRI in 1947 under Kästner. The big breakthrough was the 35BL 3 in 1980. A collective cheer was heard from cinematographers and camera assistants: it had a new PL mount, quieter operation, and no longer required a lens blimp for silent shooting. The various 35BL models worked on major features, including *Barry Lyndon* (1975, John Alcott ASC, BSC) *Taxi Driver* (1976, Michael Chapman ASC), *Apocalypse Now* (1979, Vittorio Storaro ASC, AIC) *The Shining* (1980, John Alcott ASC, BSC), *Fanny and Alexander* (1982, Sven Nykvist ASC) and many more.

1975 saw the introduction of a silent, ergonomic, shoulder-resting, coaxial magazine camera: the ARRIFLEX 16SR. Its designer, Erich Kästner, imagined the 16SR (Silent Reflex) as a documentary and newsreel 16 mm film camera so lightweight and portable that it could fit inside a custom metal and leather executive-style attaché case that any well-dressed DP would be proud to carry onboard an airplane. The camera was symmetrical, designed under the correct assumption that not everyone was right-handed, right-eyed and right-shouldered. It worked on every imaginable production, from docs and news to commercials and features, and became one of ARRI's best-selling cameras of all time.

For many ARRIFLEX camera users, ZEISS "Standard" lenses were the benchmark. They were about the size of a tennis ball; you could carry an entire set in your backpack. By the time 35BL cameras arrived in 1972, the mounts were bayonet, and it's been said that the secret to the success of the 35BL as a lightweight location camera was the set of ARRI/ZEISS Super Speed lenses introduced in 1975. To use these bayonet-mount lenses, you needed a bayonet-mount camera, which was basically unique to ARRI. With a maximum aperture of T1.4 (later T1.3), the Super Speeds enabled movies to be shot at night, on location, with practical lights and available streetlights. The first set was used on *Taxi Driver*.

In 1983 ARRI GB opened in the UK, under Derrick Ross and Paul Wild. It was here that the first dedicated marketing and sales team for ARRI lighting products was created, alongside camera sales. A rental business was later added, allowing new ARRI products to be introduced to the market, and ARRI Rental UK remains a key hub to this day.

Filmmakers had been interested in larger formats from the moment Edison and Eastman standardized the 35 mm 18x24 mm frame. For example, the Cinémathèque in Paris has in its collection a 65 mm camera from 1896 and a Lumière 75 mm camera from 1899. The ARRIFLEX 765 arrived 90 years later–in 1989. It was silent, sync sound, 2–100 fps, with an adjustable, motorized mirror shutter, and a separate motor for the camera movement, synchronized electronically to reduce noise–something unheard of at the time. This principle would be used in the next cameras, the ARRIFLEX 535 in 1990 and 435 in 1994.

Success is not assured for every endeavor, and ARRI's 535 camera did not sell in high numbers. Technically, the 535 was a marvel, with an adjustable viewfinder system for spherical, anamorphic, 100% optical or fractional video assist viewing. But crews found it big, bulky and heavy. ARRI quickly went back to the design table and released the lighter, smaller and more practical 535 B in 1993. Vittorio Storaro AIC, ASC didn't mind; in 1993 he shot *Little Buddha* with Bernardo Bertolucci using ARRIFLEX 535 and 765 cameras. Nor did Roger Deakins CBE, ASC, BSC, who liked the 535 and its coaxial magazine that he could tuck under his arm while operating on a fluid head. Roger commented, "It would be interesting to work this out–what comes first: the ambition or technology? People's ambitions for the way films can be made and the quality of the work are forever expanding, and that forces technology in new directions."

The ARRIFLEX 435 came out in 1994 as a 35 mm MOS and high-speed camera to replace the 35 III. Its dual 3-pin pull-down claws and industry-standard dual registration pins assured optical printer steadiness. Frame rates up to 150 fps could be combined with in-camera speed ramps by means of a motorized mirror shutter, and the lens iris could be coupled to a control unit. TV commercials immediately embraced the technology of speed-iris-mirror shutter control, as agency creatives, directors and DPs unleashed spates of beautiful sequences exploring time and motion.

The digital age at ARRI really began in 1995 with design work on the ARRILASER. Launched in 1998, the ARRILASER printed digital image files to film. Imagine a laser printer, but instead of paper, the printing is done on motion picture film. Originally intended for visual effects sequences, the

ARRILASER became an industry standard for printing digital intermediates of entire movies onto film and for archival black-and-white separation masters that safeguard our cinematic heritage.

Meanwhile, a filmmaker in Austria named Fritz Gabriel Bauer had been getting so involved with equipment that he founded his own company, Moviecam, to build cameras the way he liked them. ARRI acquired Moviecam in the 1990s and announced the new ARRICAM ST and LT cameras in 2000 —combining technologies from both systems. The ST was ARRI's first 35 mm silent camera with displacement magazines (instead of coaxial) and was to be the last 35 mm silent studio film camera that ARRI would design—although ARRICAMs successfully work to this day.

The ARRICAM cameras came with another new capability: LDS—a Lens Data System that displayed focus, iris, zoom and other information about the ARRI/ZEISS lens that was working in its mount. So, in the same year that the ARRICAMs were unveiled, ARRI and ZEISS began to supply Ultra Prime lenses fitted with LDS.

What was about to come came quickly. The combined influences of art, technique, technology, Moore's Law, manufacturing and marketing resulted in an acceleration of product introductions that would completely change the way movies were made. It was as if an industry accustomed to a new camera or lens perhaps once a decade was now entering warp speed, or to use a more familiar camera analogy, a speed ramp.

April 2001. ARRI Managing Director Franz Kraus raced into the central hall of the NAB exhibition in Las Vegas waving a brand-new Canon EOS D30 digital SLR with the first CMOS image sensor, which he had just purchased at a nearby big-box store. "This is the future of our industry," he proclaimed. People looked at him with the kind of disbelief with which one might greet a prediction of the end of the world. Someone asked, "How long?" He answered, "2010." Of course, he was right. Working models of the ARRI ALEXA were introduced in 2010. But we're getting ahead of the story. Franz Kraus was the visionary technologist at ARRI, with an infectious enthusiasm for image science and the way pictures looked—and a stubborn streak of perfectionism that brooked no shortcuts.

The ARRIFLEX 235 (2003) was the last 35 mm film camera ARRI would build. Many considered it to be the most elegantly styled camera of all time, with its dolphin-shaped magazine and graceful ergonomic shape. The 235 was designed as a 35 mm MOS camera to be used handheld, on stabilizers, on rigs and underwater.

The following year, the ARRISCAN came out. It had a 35 mm CMOS sensor to scan motion picture film up to 6K resolution. A new chain of events emerged. It was now called "workflow." Films could be shot on film, digitized in real time to data files, edited, graded, assembled and then printed back out to film with an ARRILASER. The invention of the ARRISCAN led to faster conversion of film images to data files. Faster speeds led to lower costs of digitizing. The result was a creative revolution in the digital age of feature films that was previously restricted to the domain of high-end commercials because of cost. Now, entire features could be affordably scanned as digital intermediates, and highly talented, rock-star colorists worked with cinematographers on grading, power windows, secondary color correction, filter effects, smoothing selected areas and so on.

The ARRIFLEX D-20 was ARRI's first digital cine camera, introduced in November 2005. It used the same CMOS sensor technology as the ARRISCAN, with a look that was indeed cinematic and a size that was familiar. It had the same aspect ratio and dimensions as traditional 35 mm film—something most other companies failed to recognize and a decision that probably assured the success of ARRI's digital endeavors that would follow. Steps for the D-20 were tentative at first. It was to be a limited quantity experiment to test the digital waters, a rental-only camera, not for sale.

ARRI and ZEISS kept developing newer lenses that raised the bar in terms of sharpness, resolution and contrast. At NAB 2005, the ARRI/ZEISS T1.3 Master Prime lenses were introduced. T-shirts proclaimed, "Breathless!" and they truly were. When you racked focus, the image did not "breathe": it did not appear to zoom or change size as you quickly focused from near to far.

At NAB 2006, ARRI showed the ARRIFLEX 416—the next (and last) generation Super 16 mm camera. It combined ARRICAM technology with the styling of a 235, in a size reminiscent of the 16SR. Someone quipped, "The analog 416

has an image area slightly larger than a 2/3-inch single-chip 2K camera, with 12 minutes of uncompressed archival-quality storage per magazine, each film frame capable of storing about 65 MB of data, and one roll holding the equivalent of about 1.123 GB." It was ARRI's last analog camera. Digital cameras were advancing faster than predicted.

But wait, not so fast. Rarely has a film looked as beautiful as *Carol* (2015), especially a film shot in Super 16. Ed Lachman ASC was the cinematographer, using an ARRIFLEX 416, with two great actresses gorgeously glowing in breathtaking light, a moving camera, motivated reflections, mirrors, flares, streaks and muted colors. The Kodak Vision3 16 mm negative was digitized with an ARRISCAN at Goldcrest and the DI was graded by John Dowdell III.

Three years after the D-20 came out, ARRI redesigned and redesignated the camera as the D-21. Still straddling the terms "experimental" and "production-ready," it was intended for TV production so as not to interfere with sales of film cameras. Like the D-20, it was a bit cumbersome, a rental item only, later reluctantly for sale, but the images were very good. By 2008, there were 56 D-21 cameras at 13 rental houses worldwide.

IBC, Amsterdam, September 2009—a pivotal moment. Some have said that ARRI bet the company on this new digital camera. The ARRI booth was very quiet, very tense in the minutes before IBC opened. Would anyone show up? Would they notice the three prototype ARRI digital camera "sisters" that were presented as wooden models, code-named ALEXA EV, ALEXA EV-Plus, and ALEXA OV-Plus? The doors to IBC Hall 11 opened at 10 a.m. Five minutes later, the ARRI team was smiling. Throngs of DPs and rental houses were swarming the booth, placing orders. By the end of the show the name "ALEXA" had caught on, and it seemed difficult to imagine calling these cameras anything else when they went into production in mid-2010.

There were a number of things in ALEXA's favor. It looked and felt like an ARRI film camera: solid, rugged, ready to endure life on location. It was easy to use. The menu and buttons seemed like old friends, not much different from an ARRICAM. Most important of all, the images had a filmlike look. The dynamic range, the range of exposure, was similar. Highlights and shadow areas could be exposed in familiar ways, using a light meter instead of a waveform monitor if you liked. It did not look like video. Somewhat later, Roger Deakins said, "This camera has brought us to a point where digital is simply better." What really mattered was that cinematographers, directors and audiences liked the way the image looked. They found it pleasing. It matched their expectations during the transition from film to digital. It was comfortable. The controls were familiar. They felt at home.

ARRI's image experts, with years of experience working in postproduction, color science and image aesthetics, had conducted extensive research on how pictures should look and what image processing would be required to achieve cinematic imagery from digital capture. As Franz Kraus explained, "People thought that because ARRI made film cameras, how could they possibly have a successful digital camera? That would have to be luck. No, it was hard work over many years, starting with the ARRILASER."

In the transition from analog technology to digital, the ARRI team had experience with film and digital cameras—the user interface, wireless control, micro controllers, CMOS sensors, FPGA-based image processing. "We had done these things before and benefitted from the 235 and 416 designs. Why should digital capture have a totally different user interface? Shooting takes place not for technical reasons but for creative ones," Franz Kraus added.

When the original ALEXA 35 mm digital camera was presented to the filmmaking community, it was positioned "for HD television, commercials and a few features," with the promise that "uncompromised and uncompressed 4K resolution will remain in the domain of 35 mm film for some time to come." That humble camera for "a few features" went on to become one of the most successful digital cine cameras of all time, capturing 80 percent of major motion picture productions by 2017.

At IBC 2010 in Amsterdam, ARRI presented prototypes of a new focusable LED Fresnel lighting fixture that promised the cool-to-the-touch and energy-efficient advantages of LED illumination with the spot-flood control and lifelike color rendition of traditional Fresnel fixtures. The ARRI L7 (L for LED and 7 for 7" Fresnel) arrived in April 2011. Available in tungsten, daylight and color-controllable versions, it was like an electric swatchbook. ARRI L5 and L10 fixtures followed.

The James Bond film *Skyfall* (2012), shot with two prototype ALEXA Studio cameras by Roger Deakins, grossed $1.1 billion worldwide. ARRI Lighting's blockbuster fixture premiered in April 2015 with an equally auspicious name: SkyPanel. It was a new line of ARRI LED soft lights, brighter than a 2 kW tungsten soft light or a 6 kW tungsten space light. About the size of a 2 kW zip light that was cool to the touch, SkyPanels could plug into the wall and produce a flattering wraparound light that actors and cinematographers loved. Like the L-Series of ARRI LED Fresnels, SkyPanel C (color) versions were fully tuneable, adjustable from 2,800 K to 10,000 K, with plus and minus green correction, vivid color selection (party colors) and saturation adjustment. With the SkyPanel, ARRI Lighting stepped into the digital age as successfully as ARRI Camera Systems did with the ALEXA. What synchronicities of digital camera and lighting equipment might the future bring? What endless creative possibilities?

Company founder August Arnold would have been pleased. He was usually ahead of the times, especially in lighting. Colleagues remember Dr. Arnold telling them for years that he had one word about the future of cinema lighting: "Daylight." His first practical implementations of daylight fixtures were early HMI units at the 1972 Munich Olympics. In 1924, ARRI built their first electric tungsten lighting fixtures with faceted mirror reflectors. A similar technology of multi-segmented mirrors would reappear 82 years later, in 2006, on the ARRIMAX 18/12 "Most Powerful HMI PAR Light on the Planet," and on subsequent M-Series fixtures.

In October 2012, August Arnold's son, Robert Arnold, sold his 50 percent stake in the company. The Stahl family, heirs of Robert Richter, now own 100 percent of ARRI. Christoph Stahl explained, "We bought Arnold's share because we didn't want to partner with a financial investor. Bobby Arnold sold because his health was deteriorating; his daughter was still quite young and not interested in continuing our partnership. The way he sold was fair and you could see that the future of our common company mattered to him." Bobby Arnold was the "face" of ARRI for many years. Most filmmakers who entered the main gate at 89 Tuerkenstrasse became friends, and evenings rarely went by where he wasn't entertaining them at one of the many Munich restaurants at which he had permanent reservations.

There was another big announcement in the final months of 2012: ARRI/ ZEISS Master Anamorphic lenses. Because of ALEXA's industry-standard 4:3 sensor and 18 mm image height, the feel, myth and reality of the legendary anamorphic look had been enticing DPs since the camera's introduction. The new ARRI/ZEISS Master Anamorphic prime lenses were a combined effort of the long design, technical and marketing partnership between Munich and Oberkochen.

ARRI Rental launched the ALEXA 65 at Cinec in September 2014. Within the next 25 months, ALEXA 65 cameras worked on more 65 mm productions than had been shot in the previous 25 years. Continuing ARRI's involvement with this iconic larger format where the 765 left off, the ALEXA 65 has now been taken up in earnest by the world's leading filmmakers. One early adopter was Emmanuel Lubezki ASC, AMC, who combined it with ALEXA Mini and ALEXA XT on *The Revenant* (2015). A year earlier, Lubezki had gracefully glided an ALEXA M through *Birdman* (2014). He noted, "Handheld cameras, especially smaller ones like the ARRI ALEXA M, allow you to get really, really close to the actors. You can move within their space and between them. It allows you to get into the eye of the hurricane, as we say. It was inconvenient timing that the ALEXA Mini wasn't ready for *Birdman*. But we were able to work with the ALEXA M very nicely. To me what is important, and what I wish for, is that we have many brushes, many different tools to tell stories and express emotion in different ways."

Dr. Jörg Pohlman joined ARRI in 2014 as Managing Director. He commented, "If we think about the 100 years of ARRI, look at where we are and where we want to be in the future, one of the key factors is how unique a company it is. We are involved in almost all aspects of the motion picture industry, from developing cameras, lighting and accessories, to product manufacturing, including sensor bonding. Our ARRI Rental Group gives us proximity to film sets, and provides immediate feedback if something does not work or can be improved. When you finish shooting, you can come back to ARRI Media for postproduction, editing, sound, VFX, mixing, DI and distribution. ARRI can provide the entire process from developing a camera all the way to releasing feature films into theaters. I think that makes ARRI unique."

In the introduction to his book *From Méliès to 3D: the Machines of Cinema*, Laurent Mannoni, Director and Conservator of la Cinémathèque Française, wrote, "Cinema offers an eclectic mixture of technology and artistic sensibility that often allows the production of major and surprising works. Digital, even with its volatility and propensity to devour everything, opens up exciting prospects. What matters is that the cinema, the writing of movement, born in prehistoric caves, remains very much alive as an art today. The cinema, as Abel Gance said, must always be reinvented."

The cinema has been reinvented over and over again. For a hundred years, ARRI has created the tools and technology that enabled filmmakers to find new ways to tell their stories with moving images. Styles evolved, techniques changed, reacting and in reaction to the art and tools that brought cinematographers, some skeptical, others thrilled as an audience on opening night, along a century's trajectory from studios to locations, from silent to sound, from analog to digital.

Endurance is elusive in the pursuit of cinematographic dreams. As the director said in François Truffaut's *Day for Night* (1973), "Shooting a film is like a stagecoach ride in the Wild West. In the beginning, you hope for a pleasant journey, but pretty soon, you begin to wonder if you'll reach the destination." Providing the tools to tell those stories is also risky business requiring resilience. As successful merchants of the means to those dreams, ARRI has provided the tools and services of cinema production for one hundred years, collecting an impressive 19 Academy Sci-Tech Awards along the way. A company founded by two friends has grown to a team of 1,400, some of whom are third-generation employees–truly a family concern. And the adventure continues. ARRI's centennial celebrates the company and the thousands of cinematographers, filmmakers, rental houses and production crews who work with the things that ARRI provides. If there is one comprehensive explanation for ARRI's longevity, it is their foresight and acumen to listen to customers, friends and colleagues. Those words continue to resonate in the following pages.

rmans as household help. **1941** **01-01-1941**: Jews are no longer allowed to hire Germans as household help. **08-01-**
'Jews not welcome' must be placed in cafes and restaurants. Owners are forced to comply by members of the
1: individuals with at least one Jewish grandparent are required to update their entry in the municipal population
verview of where Jews live. **23-01-1941**: Jewish students are no longer eligible for government financial aid available
e paramilitary WA and the Dutch SS vandalise the office of The Hague's Jewish religious congregation. **05-02-1941**:
ish descent. **08-02-1941**: in Amsterdam's busy nightlife area Rembrandtplein, WA members provoke fights in cafes
y into cafe-cabaret Alcazar where Jewish artists regularly perform. The interior is smashed to pieces. **11-02-1941**:
ir studies must apply no later than 31 March. **11-02-1941**: at the outdoor market on Waterlooplein in Amsterdam's
om other neighbourhoods. During this fight, a WA member is fatally wounded. **12-02-1941**: in response to a number
man authorities, a Jewish Council is established in Amsterdam. Diamond merchant Abraham Asscher and Professor
alls on Amsterdam's Jewish residents to hand in their weapons. **19-02-1941**: the German police raid the Amsterdam
h a substance, that causes nasty burns. **21-02-1941**: suspended Jewish civil servants are officially dismissed. A total
ntually 3,400 in France. **22 and 23-02-1941**: the first major *razzia* – a violent raid – against Jews living in Amsterdam's
e cream parlour. Young men between the ages of 20 and 35 are forcibly rounded up in the streets or removed from
sterdam. **25-02-1941**: this *razzia* is the breaking point, resulting in a massive protest strike in Amsterdam and cities
ut down by the German police. Nine people are killed and dozens injured. **27-02-1941**: Jews may no longer donate
ring the *razzia* earlier in the month, 389 are deported to Buchenwald concentration camp. **28-02-1941**: in retaliation
ts in Amsterdam, Hilversum and Zaandam must close at 8 pm. After 8:30 pm, a curfew is enforced. **28-02-1941**: the
iations and foundations. **03-03-1941**: the first execution on Dutch soil takes place on Waalsdorpervlakte near The
announce how the required registration of people who are entirely or partly of Jewish descent will take place. The
unishment for failing to comply. **12-03-1941**: a large Nazi rally is held in the Concertgebouw, Amsterdam's renowned
h people. **12-03-1941**: companies owned by Jews are liquidated or taken over by non-Jews. **13-03-1941**: a group of
teen members of the '*Geuzen*' resistance group. **20-03-1941**: all Jewish associations and foundations are disbanded.
oards of Jewish religious congregations. **20-03-1941**: supervised by Willy Lages and Klaus Barbie of the Nazi security
1934, young German refugees have been trained in agricultural and technical occupations here. Most of them are
n practicing liberal professions that require taking an oath. **31-03-1941**: the *Zentralstelle für jüdische Auswanderung*,
e forced emigration of Jews from the Netherlands. It also becomes responsible for confiscating Jewish property and
city's parks. **11-04-1941**: by order of the German occupier the first issue of a Jewish weekly, *Het Joodsche Weekblad*,
pier and must also publish announcements issued by the occupation authority. **15-04-1941**: Jews must hand in their
ven the municipal administration and police receive no instructions on this matter, the measure is not enforced
wish doctors, dentists, pharmacists, midwives, notaries, lawyers, translators and interpreters may now only have
n, The Hague and Rotterdam. **06-05-1941**: a number of streets in Amsterdam are designated as Jewish. Signs are
canal). The neighbourhood is referred to as the *Judenviertel/Joodsche wijk* (Jewish quarter). **07-05-1941**: Sybren Tulp,
issuing of identity cards begins. At a later date, the IDs of Jews will be stamped on both sides with a capital letter J.
in retaliation for the February strike are deported from Buchenwald to Mauthausen concentration camp. In the
before 3 June. Jewish landowners must sell their property before 1 September. **31-05-1941**: the establishment of the
-1941: Jews may no longer use public swimming pools, go to the beach or swim in the sea. **31-05-1941**: Jews may no
rdwijk, Zandvoort and Bergen. **31-05-1941**: Jews may no longer attend the horse races. **11-06-1941**: in retaliation for
are taken to Schoorl internment camp. Included among them are nearly 60 former residents of the farming village
w months. **19-06-1941**: in Utrecht, Jews are prohibited from frequenting certain public places. The city's police are
ermany begins its assault on the Soviet Union. In the newly-occupied territories, Jewish men and communists are
f Shabbat on Saturday, Jews were allowed to open their shops on Sunday. From now on this is forbidden. **25-07-1941**:
aganda or listening to the radio illegally. The highest-ranking SS officer in the Netherlands, Hanns Albin Rauter, is
07-1941: announcement of new rules on keeping pigeons. Jews are no longer allowed to practice this pastime. The
ith preparing the solution to the 'Jewish Question' in Europe. **01-08-1941**: Jewish estate agents may no longer have

non-Jewish clients. **01-08-1941**: the Jewish farming village in the Wieringermeer polder is permanently shut down. The last residents are taken to Amsterdam. **08-08-1941**: the German authorities seize the Amsterdam Jewish bank Lippmann, Rosenthal & Co. (LiRo) for the purpose of looting Jewish assets. Jews must register their bank balances and other valuable possessions here. Any balances over 1,000 Dutch guilders must be transferred to this bank. **11-08-1941**: Jews must officially register any land and real estate they own. **11-08-1941**: under the code name 14f13, the first prisoners from Mauthausen are gassed at Hartheim Castle in Austria. Almost all of them are Dutch Jews. The 14f13 programme stems from '*Aktion T4*', which began in 1939. As part of this 'purification programme', people whom the Nazis considered disabled were killed or sterilised. **01-09-1941**: Jewish students are prohibited from attending the same schools as non-Jewish students. Therefore, Jewish schools are set up where all the personnel are also Jewish. Since Amsterdam has a large Jewish population, implementing this measure is delayed until 1 October. **03, 04 and 05-09-1941**: experiments gassing prisoners are carried out in Auschwitz. A total of 600 Russian prisoners of war and some 250 sick prisoners, most of them Polish, are murdered. **14-09-1941**: during *razzias* in the Dutch cities of Enschede, Hengelo, Almelo and Oldenzaal, 103 Jewish young men are rounded up. Two days later, they are all deported to Mauthausen. Within four months, they are all murdered. **15-09-1941**: Jews are not allowed to attend public meetings and events. By now outdoor markets, restaurants, hotels, guesthouses, parks, sport fields, zoos, theatres, cabarets, concerts, museums, libraries, reading rooms and cinemas are 'Prohibited for Jews'. This is clearly indicated by signs. **16-09-1941**: if Jews want to travel, they must apply for a permit from the *Zentralstelle*. **18-09-1941**: the savings accounts of German Jews living in the Netherlands are confiscated. **22-09-1941**: Jews are no longer welcome at non-profit associations and foundations. **07 and 08-10-1941**: during *razzias* in the Achterhoek, a region in the east of the Netherlands, and in the cities of Apeldoorn, Arnhem and Zwolle, 70 Jewish men are rounded up. They are deported to Mauthausen. All of them are murdered within two months. **08-10-1941**: Seyss-Inquart decides that German anti-Jewish policymaking should be separated into policing and non-policing measures. Non-policing measures are meant to exclude Jews from social and economic life. Policing measures include direct preparations for the mass deportation of Jews, meaning their physical removal from the Netherlands. **10-10-1941**: the underground press reports that around 700 Jewish men have been deported to Mauthausen. Of that group, 300 men are rumoured to have perished. Both figures turn out to be significantly higher. **10-10-1941**: labour camps are set up in the Netherlands for unemployed Jewish men. **14-10-1941**: the start of '*Aktion Reinhard*'. As a part of this, in the months to come, the extermination camps Belzec, Treblinka and Sobibor are built in occupied Poland. The purpose of these camps is to kill Jews as quickly and efficiently as possible by using gas. **20-10-1941**: the Jewish Council must create a comprehensive card index with detailed information about all the Jews in the Netherlands. **22-10-1941**: any kind of paid work done by Jews can be subject to permits or other conditions. Paid work can also be forbidden. **22-10-1941**: non-Jews may no longer do any work in Jewish homes. **22-10-1941**: Jews may no longer publish articles in trade magazines. **27-10-1941**: the Jewish Council in Amsterdam is required to expand its activities to the rest of the Netherlands. All future contact between Jews from the provinces and the occupation authorities must now go via Amsterdam. Unlike similar Jewish councils in Belgium, France and Germany, the council in the Netherlands has no official status. **01-11-1941**: Jews may no longer be members of organisations with non-Jewish members. This includes sport clubs and music ensembles. Jewish university students are expelled from student societies. **01-11-1941**: the professional licenses of 1,600 Jews are revoked. **03-11-1941**: three playgrounds in Amsterdam are set up as outdoor markets for Jews. **07-11-1941**: Jews are no longer welcome in bridge, dance and tennis clubs. **07-11-1941**: Jews may now only travel or relocate with a *Zentralstelle* permit, which must now be requested via the Jewish Council. **10-11-1941**: the *Joodse Coördinatie Commissie* – a steering committee set up by-and-for the Dutch Jewish community under German occupation – is disbanded by the authorities, barely a year after its establishment. **25-11-1941**: to continue working in their professions, artists, architects, writers, journalists, musicians and actors must join the *Kultuurkamer*, a Nazi-sponsored cultural association. Jews are banned from joining. Also, anyone married to or living with a Jew may not become a member. As of spring 1942, membership is mandatory. **25-11-1941**: German Jews lose their citizenship. This includes German Jews who have emigrated or fled to the Netherlands. **05-12-1941**: all non-Dutch Jews must register with the *Zentralstelle* for 'voluntary emigration'. **07-12-1941**: Japan attacks the US Naval Base at Pearl Harbor in Hawaii. A day later, the London Cabinet – Dutch government-in-exile – declares war on Japan. **1942** **01-01-1942**: formation of the *Wachbataillon Nordwest* comprised of 600 members of the Dutch SS. This battalion guards different Dutch concentration camps and prisons, such as Camp Amersfoort. **01-01-1942**: a member of the NSB is appointed Director-General of the PTT (Dutch postal, telegram and telephone service). Inside the organisation, he grooms an entire network of informers. **05-01-1942**: the Jewish Council is ordered to call up 1,400 unemployed Jewish men from Amsterdam for health checks. They will be sent to labour camps in the province of Drenthe on 10 January. **07-01-1942**: local employment agencies in the Netherlands are ordered to call up unemployed Jewish men in their regions for health checks. On 20 January Jews from areas outside of Amsterdam will be sent to labour camps in the province of Groningen. **08 and 09-01-1942**: to meet the quota of unemployed Jewish men to be deployed to labour camps in the Netherlands, the selling of goods outdoors is made illegal in Amsterdam. Jewish market vendors and street peddlers find themselves out of work. They are rounded up in the streets. **10-01-1942**: the first 905 Jewish unemployed men are sent to a labour camp in the province of Drenthe. **11-01-1942**: the Imperial Japanese Army invades the Dutch East Indies, then a colony of the Netherlands, now Indonesia. **12-01-1942**: German regulations, ordinances and decrees may no longer be tested against existing Dutch laws. **17-01-1942**: a total of 172 Jews from the city of Zaandam must move to Amsterdam. And 98 stateless Jews leave for Westerbork, which functions as a refugee camp. They may only bring the baggage they can carry. Their remaining possessions are confiscated. Mix married Jewish couples must relocate to Amsterdam with all their belongings. **20-01-1942**: a second group of unemployed Jews from Amsterdam leaves for labour camps in Drenthe and Groningen. In the months to come thousands more will follow. **20-01-1942**: in a villa on Lake Wannsee on the outskirts of Berlin, representatives of the German ministries and SS discuss the '*Endlösung der Judenfrage*', the 'final solution to the Jewish Question'. Participants at this meeting hear in misleading language what 'employment of the Jews in the East' involves. The harsh reality is heavy-forced labour, beatings, starvation, gassing and executions. Also discussed is the fate of Jews married to non-Jews (mixed marriages) and their offspring. **23-01-1942**: the identity cards of Jews must be stamped with a capital letter J. **25-01-1942**: a total of 137 stateless Jews from the city of Hilversum must leave for Westerbork refugee camp. They may only bring the baggage they can carry. **31-01-1942**: Jews lose their severance pay protection. Instead of unemployment benefits, employers may pay out a lump sum. **02-02-1942**: department IV B4 of the German security police is established in The Hague. This unit is tasked with preparing and organising the deportation of the Jews from the Netherlands. **09-02-1942**: a total of 150 stateless Jews from the city of Utrecht must leave for Westerbork refugee camp. Included among them are 30 orphans. **13-02-1942**: the Jewish Council in Amsterdam is ordered to arrange 3,000 more Jewish men to be sent to labour camps. The council refuses. **17-02-1942**: Seyss-Inquart informs representatives of churches protesting the persecution of the Jews that their compassion is misplaced. **17-02-1942**: Jews are no longer welcome in waiting rooms and dining areas of train stations. They are only allowed on the platforms. **04-03-1942**: representatives of the occupation authorities in the Netherlands, Belgium and France are summoned to Berlin. There a decision is taken that Jews must wear a visible form of identification in public. **05-03-1942**: the Jewish Council in Amsterdam is ordered to call up Jewish men even if they still have jobs. They will be sent to labour camps in the

Netherlands. **06-03-1942**: discussions take place in Berlin about the sterilisation of specific groups of Jews in mixed marriages and those with less than three Jewish grandparents. **09-03-1942**: the Royal Netherlands East Indies Army capitulates. Japan occupies the Dutch East Indies. Prisoners of war and civilians with European backgrounds are placed in internment camps. **15-03-1942**: as part of '*Aktion Reinhard*', the deportation and murder of Poland's Jews in extermination camps begins. **17-03-1942**: in the southeast of occupied Poland, Belzec extermination camp goes into operation. **20-03-1942**: Jews may not remove furniture, household goods or any other belongings from their homes. This applies especially to Jews who are forced to relocate to Amsterdam. **20-03-1942**: Jews may no longer drive automobiles. **25-03-1942**: Jews may no longer marry non-Jews or have sexual relations with them. Dozens of Jewish men are arrested for officially registering their intent to marry non-Jewish women. By doing this, they are considered guilty of 'racial shame'. **26-03-1942**: Jews from the cities and towns of Alkmaar, Beverwijk, Bloemendaal, Den Helder, IJmuiden, Santpoort and Zandvoort must move to Amsterdam. They may only bring the baggage they can carry. **27-03-1942**: the first deportation train from Western Europe leaves for Auschwitz concentration and extermination camp. This train departs from France. Aboard are 1,112 Jews. Within three months, ninety percent of them are killed as a result of harsh forced labour. **01-04-1942**: in various Dutch cities, Jewish patients are transferred from non-Jewish hospitals to Jewish hospitals. **02-04-1942**: Jews are no longer allowed to register their intent to marry at Amsterdam's city hall or to get married there. **11-04-1942**: signs stating 'Forbidden for Jews' are removed by a boy in Leeuwarden. In retaliation, ten Jewish men from the city are arrested and taken to Camp Amersfoort. Some of them perish there. The rest are later murdered in other camps. **16-04-1942**: the Nazis loot the diamond exchange in Amsterdam, confiscating over 70,000 carats in diamonds – the equivalent of eighty percent of the Dutch inventory. **23-04-1942**: the Jewish Council is ordered to arrange health checks for 1,000 Jewish men to be deployed to labour camps in the Netherlands. Jewish doctors reject as many of them as possible. **25-04-1942**: propaganda distributed by the NSB encourages the deportation of the Jews. Their weekly newspaper *Volk en Vaderland* (People and Fatherland) refers to Jews as 'a deadly national danger' and calls for their elimination from society. **28-04-1942**: violators of anti-Jewish regulations are punished. If they receive prison sentences longer than six weeks, they are sent to Mauthausen. This is equivalent to the death penalty. **29-04-1942**: an announcement that from 3 May every Jew age six and older must wear a yellow six-pointed star – with the word 'Jood' (Jew) printed in the middle – visible on their clothing. **30-04-1942**: the three largest Dutch trade unions are merged into the *Nederlandsche Arbeidsfront*, a Nazi-affiliated labour union established by decree. Jews are banned from being members. **01-05-1942**: Jews may not wear any kind of honorary medals, ribbons or other insignias. **03-05-1942**: in occupied Poland, the Sobibor extermination camp goes into operation. **11-05-1942**: the Jewish Council must designate 3,000 Jewish men to be deployed to labour camps. **12-05-1942**: Jews may no longer have postal banking accounts, a widely used service available via post offices. Account holders must declare in writing whether they are Jewish. **15-05-1942**: an announcement that the yellow star must be visibly worn by Jews in courtyards, gardens and even standing in a front doorway opening. **18-05-1942**: German SS commander Heinrich Himmler inspects the newly established *Politiebataljon Amsterdam*. This battalion will later actively engage in removing Jews from their homes. **21-05-1942**: by 30 June Jews must surrender art objects, gold, silver, precious stones and pearls to the banking institute Lippmann, Rosenthal & Co., which confiscates Jewish assets. This also applies to cash, money orders, stocks and savings accounts of more than 250 Dutch guilders. The maximum amount of cash a Jewish family may have at home is reduced from 1,000 to 250 guilders per month. **21-05-1942**: Jews must declare horses, vehicles and boats in writing to the *Zentralstelle* by 30 June. **26-05-1942**: establishment of the *Vrijwillige Hulppolitie*, an auxiliary police unit comprised of volunteers. Mainly members of the NSB and the Dutch SS are admitted to its ranks. From 1943, they will be deployed to remove Jews from their